BRASS HEAVENS
Reasons for Unanswered Prayer

Paul Tautges
Cruciform Press | January

For Karen,
the most loving, supportive, and patient wife
any husband could ever hope to receive
from the Lord.
"Her children rise up and call her blessed;
her husband also, and he praises her:
'Many women have done excellently,
but you surpass them all.'"
(Proverbs 31:28-29)

- Paul Tautges

CruciformPress

CruciformPress.com | info@CruciformPress.com

"Some things in the Scriptures are conveniently ignored—such as the reality that there might be things in our lives that would cause a breakdown in our prayers being heard and answered by God. But this book will not let us continue to bury Scripture's clear teaching, or continue to ignore the ongoing rebellions, unrelinquished resentments, and unconfessed sins in our lives that may be hindering our prayers."

Nancy Guthrie, author, *Seeing Jesus in the Old Testament* series

"Few things vex the Christian more than unanswered prayer. Paul Tautges scatters the darkness of our doubts with six reasons for unanswered prayer. He blends biblical teaching with many practical illustrations to challenge and comfort us when the heavens seem as brass. Read this to revive your prayers, to melt the heavens, and to increase your answers."

David Murray, Puritan Reformed Theological Seminary

"Paul Tautges has a lucid and practical style that helps the believer to deal thoughtfully with his prayer life. Both motivating and convicting, here is a very useful and biblical probe for examining and excising those sins that are hindrances to believing prayer. Read and obey for the sake of your future, your family, and the work of God in the world."

Jim Elliff, founder, Christian Communicators Worldwide

"In *Brass Heavens*, pastor-shepherd-author Paul Tautges addresses the age-old question: Why do some prayers go unanswered? Wisely, Pastor Tautges grounds his answer in the character of our Triune God whose very nature is to share generously his good gifts. Tautges builds a biblical structure upon that foundation, explaining scriptural reasons for unanswered prayer. Some of these are not easy to hear—because they call us to accountability—but all are important to understand. Like the Scriptures, Tautges does not leave us in the pit of despair, but shows that where sin abounds, grace superabounds—there are biblical pathways for dealing with our role in unanswered prayers and for responding humbly to God's affectionate sovereignty in response to our prayers."

Dr. Bob Kellemen, Exec. Dir., Biblical Counseling Coalition

"One of the most painful things about the Christian life is waiting. What do we do while anguish piles up and God remains silent to our prayers? We don't need platitudes or shrugs of theological ignorance. When we walk in darkness we need to cling to our God. Paul Tautges searches the Scriptures to unveil the character and purposes of the God who is always drawing the praying Christian deeper into faith and repentance. This book shows that unanswered prayer is an opportunity for rich spiritual growth—even when the heavens are as brass."

Dr. Joel R. Beeke, Puritan Reformed Theological Seminary

"For over two decades I have been blessed to have Paul Tautges as my friend. His love for and dependency upon the Word of God, and his confessional way of applying its principles to the present realities of life, have given countless people encouragement and help. In my own life, I have come to the conclusion that the greatest work we do is on our knees. This book gives us practical ways of understanding and working through the things that hinder that indispensable work. You will be blessed as you read."

Dr. Matt Olson, President, Northland International University

"Paul Tautges opens our eyes to the mystery of talking and listening to God as he clearly communicates the reason God hears our prayers—and the reason(s) he is (or seems) silent. This short book is deeply saturated with Bible, gospel, and graceful application. It serves as a wonderful 'hearing-aid' of clarity, hope and understanding for all who have encountered brass heavens in the silence of God and have wondered, 'Is God listening?'"

Greg Lucas, author, *Wrestling With an Angel: A Story of Love, Disability, and the Lessons of Grace*

Cruciform Press

something new in Christian publishing

Our Books: Short. Clear. Concise. Helpful. Inspiring. Gospel-focused. *Print; 3 ebook formats.*

Consistent Prices: Every book costs the same.

Subscription Options: Print books or ebooks delivered to you on a set schedule, at a discount. Or buy print books or ebooks individually.

Pre-paid or Recurring Subscriptions

Print Book	$6.49 each
Ebook	$3.99 each

Non-Subscription Sales

1-5 Print Books	$8.45 each
6-50 Print Books	$7.45 each
More than 50 Print Books	$6.45 each
Single Ebooks (bit.ly/CPebks)	$5.45 each

Brass Heavens: Reasons for Unanswered Prayer

Print / PDF ISBN:	978-1-936760-63-3
ePub ISBN:	978-1-936760-65-7
Mobipocket ISBN:	978-1-936760-64-0

Table of Contents

INTRODUCTION

Right or wrong, God-centered or self-centered, there are many reasons we pray. Some pray because we view it as a means of relieving guilty feelings, or as a mystical pathway to inner peace. Others pray out of religious duty, believing that the quantity or quality of our prayers will earn God's favor and thus the attention of his ear. Still others pray from godly motives, as the fruit of a living relationship with God.

But there is another, more foundational reason we pray. We desire to be heard.

This is part of our make-up, part of our design as relational beings made in the image of God. We talk to other people because we want them to actually listen to us; we dare to open our hearts in the hope that our deepest thoughts might be verbalized, heard, and understood. The longing is so persistent that we keep trying, even when others repeatedly fail to listen.

So it is with prayer. We cry out to God because we expect him to listen. At least, we hope he will.

Sometimes our faith is feeble, and all we can scrape up is a thin hope that God *might* listen. Like the writers of certain Psalms; we cry out to God with more desperation than expectation. "Hear a just cause, O LORD; attend to my cry! Give ear to my prayer" (Psalm 17:1). "Give ear to my prayer, O God, and hide not yourself from my plea for mercy! Attend to me, and answer me" (Psalm 55:1-2). The psalmist, distressed at the prospect of God's absence, begs him to be present, attentive, and responsive. A shred of faith keeps him praying, but deep down he fears that God will not hear him—perhaps even that God cannot hear him.

The Sound of Rain

Deafness is a trial our family knows something about. Four of our ten children are hearing-impaired. For three of them the impairment was diagnosed within a few weeks after birth. But for our first son, born before the advent of mandatory newborn screening, a medical diagnosis took more than two years. Well before then, as his parents, we knew he could not hear, and it deeply pained us. But when countless tests failed to uncover a cause for the impairment, our pain grew worse. Without an obvious medical condition there was nothing to treat, and some professionals even doubted our son was actually deaf. We wanted to do everything in our power to help our son—to make it possible for him to hear the Word of God and succeed in a hearing world, but what more could we do to make the professionals understand?

Finally, the providential hand of God led us to an audiologist who diagnosed our son's sensorineural hearing loss, producing our first real glimmer of medical hope. Having identified a cause there was now a blessed solution in view. Our son needed hearing aids.

It sounds simple enough but our meager medical coverage, combined with my status then as a full-time college student and part-time hardware store manager, put the expense well out of our reach. But God is faithful even when we are faithless (2 Timothy 2:13). Graciously, our heavenly Father provided for that first pair of hearing aids through the generous giving of the fellow believers at our local church. Our two-year old son was fitted for his first ear molds within a month.

We will never forget those early days when our son began to hear.

On the way home from the audiologist's office, our son's first pair of aids resting nicely on his ears, we stopped at a humongous toy store to get him something to help celebrate this moment. We walked across the parking lot through a gentle but steady rain, entered the store, and sat our son in a shopping cart as an aid to regulating his zeal. My wife and I didn't even notice the sound of rain on the metal roof.

Our son did. As we walked up one aisle and down another, it was almost as if there were no toys on the shelves clamoring for his attention. From his perch in the shopping cart, he kept looking at the ceiling, then at me, then back at the ceiling. Finally I got it. I had been completely missing the sign language that so obviously said, "Dad, what is that amazing *noise?*"

A few days later my wife watched our little guy walk around the kitchen, clearly on some kind of mission. He went from cabinet to cabinet, to the dishwasher, to the stove, stopping briefly to touch each one, wait a moment, and move on. Finally, his face glowing with satisfaction, his hands found the source of the faint hum he could hear but hadn't been able to locate. The vibration of the refrigerator. Our son could hear!

The Heavens as Brass

Sometimes we're tempted to wonder if God can hear. After months or even years of praying over a particular person or situation, we look for evidence God is getting our message or even paying attention, and we can't find much. Why is that? Why do the heavens sometimes seem like brass? Doesn't God love us and care for us? Isn't he all-powerful?

The phrase *brass heavens* has its origins in the Pentateuch, the first five books of the Old Testament. It was part of God's warning to his chosen people Israel, a promised consequence of neglecting to obey his commands. As the nation prepared to enter the Promised Land, we find this among the curses for disobedience given by Moses: "And thy heaven that is over thy head shall be brass, and the earth that is under thee shall be iron" (Deuteronomy 28:23; KJV). Most recent translations use "bronze" instead of "brass," but the meaning is the same.

Admittedly, this verse in its context has nothing to do with prayer. Rather, it is a warning from God that periods of drought would be one of the many consequences of Israel's rebellion. The skies would appear promising, but the heavy layer of clouds would bring forth no rain. As a result, the ground would dry up and become like iron, impossible to cultivate. For a society that survived largely by agriculture, this was nothing short of a disaster.

So while the verse is not about prayer, *brass heavens* nevertheless became a common expression among Christians because it describes so well the silence of God—the drought of unanswered prayer and the famine-like spiritual unfruitfulness that believers sometimes experience. Like the people who originally adapted the phrase, I'm just using it in this book as an analogy.

The subtitle of this book reveals its larger purpose. We want to search the Scriptures for some of the reasons God appears to go silent. As we examine some causes of unanswered prayer, we will also discover the biblical means by which we may open God's ears to our voice once again.

God has a good and holy purpose for these periods of silence. He wants to test our faith that we might see for ourselves just how weak and dependent we are on him for all good things. His goal is nothing less than to heighten our spiritual sensitivities in order to draw us into more intimate fellowship and faithful obedience with him.

Prayer goes unanswered because God knows our needs far better than we understand our desires. So it is only appropriate that we spend the first two chapters of *Brass Heavens* thinking about the nature of this God to whom we pray.

Part One

THE GOD WHO HEARS, KNOWS, AND LOVES

One

THE TRIUNE GOD HEARS AND KNOWS

In prayer we tell God nothing he does not already know. Instead, our prayers acknowledge our awareness of something he has always known and that we regularly forget—that we need him and cannot live without him. As we set out to explore the causes of unanswered prayer, we must begin by understanding this God to whom we pray and on whom we depend.

Our God is triune, a unity of three persons, with each person playing a role in our every act of prayer.

- **Father.** Prayer touches the tenderness of the heavenly Father's heart like nothing else, bringing him delight as he comes to the aid of his children (Matthew 7:11).
- **Son.** Each time we pray we demonstrate our dependence on Jesus Christ, the spotless Lamb of God, who is the way, truth, and life—the only way to the Father (John 14:6).

- **Spirit.** The Holy Spirit carries our prayers to the Father's throne of grace, interpreting our heart's unutterable longings (Romans 8:26).

This is the God who knows us and our struggles far better than we do ourselves. If we are to understand anything about unanswered prayer, we must begin with him.

The Father Delights to Listen and Knows Our Needs

The first person of the Trinity—the one who freely chose to send his only Son to die for our sins—is aware of our needs, listens to our cries, and delights to give us what is good for us.

The Father Cares Enough to Listen

The man who penned Psalm 116 had a deep hope and confidence in God's love and concern for him. "I love the LORD, because he has heard my voice and my pleas for mercy. Because he inclined his ear to me, therefore I will call on him as long as I live" (Psalm 116:1-2). This psalmist answers the question, "Why pray?" with simple transparency, as if to say, "Because God hears. Because he cares enough to listen."

That may sound too simple or even a bit selfish, but the testimony is true. God's listening ear motivated this man to open his heart to God in prayer. His admission is simple, raw, and emotional. His honesty is naked. "I love God because he hears me. And because he hears me, I pray."

When my 3-year-old son is sobbing and wants to tell me what happened, I not only listen, but I also bend down to look into his eyes. So it is with the God of the universe. We may think of our prayers as feeble attempts to reach *up* to God, but when we pray, God actually *lowers* himself. "Because he inclined his ear to me, therefore I will call on him as long as I live" (v 2). The word "inclined" means "bended down." God bends down, turns his head, and listens to our cries for help.

If that is not powerful incentive to pray, then I don't know what is! God is not far away, but "near to the brokenhearted and saves the crushed in spirit" (Psalm 34:18). He is like a father who "shows compassion to his children" (Psalm 103:13). This fatherly bending down of our God and King reinforced the psalmist's confidence in God as the one who listens. Therefore he resolved, "I will call on him as long as I live."

Remarkably, as much as the confidence of this Old Testament saint should encourage us to pray, the intimacy of the New Testament's more explicit presentation of God as the Father surpasses it. He is not only the God who cares enough to listen, but he also knows everything about us and finds delight in giving good gifts to those whom he predestined for adoption through Jesus Christ (Ephesians 1:5).

The Father Knows Our Needs

While teaching his disciples about prayer, Jesus made this amazing statement: "Your Father knows what you need before you ask him" (Matthew 6:8).

Your Father. The first thing to notice here is that Jesus does not call the first person of the Trinity "the Father of heaven and earth," though that surely is true. Instead he stresses the relational aspect, saying "*your* Father." The believer in Christ has a relationship with God that the unbeliever does not. God is the Father of all in the sense that he is the Creator "from whom are all things" (1 Corinthians 8:6), but he is Father, relationally, only to believers. This relationship, which is based on grace alone through faith in Christ alone, deepens and thrives when we take our needs to the Father in prayer.

Before you ask. The second part of Jesus' comment—that our Father "knows what you need before you ask him"—can easily raise an honest question: If God already knows our needs and the always-faithful Father has promised to meet them, why bother to pray? It may seem like an obvious question, perhaps with an obvious answer, but what happens next in the gospel account is striking. Notice what Jesus *didn't* do after informing us about the Father's foreknowledge: he didn't just stop talking! If he had, we might conclude prayer is unnecessary—God knows what you need; end of story. But Jesus refused to leave us to our own flawed, finite human logic. Instead, going against our logic, our Lord said essentially the opposite: "Your Father knows what you need before you ask him. Pray then like this: 'Our Father in heaven …'"

Your loving Father knows what you need before you ask him, therefore … ask him? Jesus wants us to see that prayer is more about changing us than it is about informing God or moving him to action.

As a sacrifice of time and energy that could have been used for other things, prayer is an act of worship, one by which our hearts are exercised in faith, not merely in religious ritual. "Ask," Jesus tells us, "just ask." Why? Because true prayer cultivates humility. It requires us to acknowledge our helplessness. We ask because Jesus told us to ask. We ask because all that is good comes from God, not from our own efforts.

As we build a lifestyle of prayer, this regular acknowledgment of God's fatherly provision is infinitely more valuable than anything else we may receive. The main thing is not that in the future we might get what we pray for. The main thing is that in the present, as we pray, our greatest need is already being met. That need is the transforming work of God in our hearts, with prayer itself as one of God's appointed means of meeting that need. When Jesus promised a "reward" for those who pray in secret (Matthew 6:6), perhaps this refining work of God in our hearts is at least partly what he had in mind.

The Father Delights to Give Gifts

Having taken joy in hearing the cries of our needy hearts and knowing our needs better than we do, God delights to give us those things that will be best for us. "Every good gift and every perfect gift is from above, coming down from the Father of lights with whom there is no variation or shadow due to change" (James 1:17). Written by James, the half-brother of Jesus, this verse portrays God in a way that should powerfully motivate us to pray.

Good and perfect gifts. God is the source of all that is good, and he delights in giving good things to his children. Jesus says in Luke 11:13, "If you then, who are evil, know how to give good gifts to your children, how much more will the heavenly Father give the Holy Spirit to those who ask him!" If we as human beings find joy in giving our children what we believe to be good gifts, how much more does an infinitely good God know how to give to his children! Sometimes we think God withholds things from us because he does not love us. The opposite is true. Sometimes God's withholding of our requests proves his love. He did exactly this for the apostle Paul to keep his pride in check (2 Corinthians 12:7-9). God loves us too much to let us go down a harmful path, even if we see it as the path of blessing.

Father of lights. All of these undeserved gifts come down from the "Father of lights," the creator of the sun, moon, and stars (Genesis 1:14). These heavenly bodies testify to God's glory in part by offering a visual representation of God's "light"—his holiness and purity (1 John 1:5). Men, however, are not light—we naturally love darkness because we love sin (John 3:19). But it is impossible for God to be involved in darkness in any way whatsoever. There is "no variation or shadow due to change" in God for he is pure light—unchanging and unchangeable. Unlike the sun, moon, and stars, the light of God's holiness never surges or fades. It always burns with the same infinite intensity. Therefore it is impossible for God to tempt us toward evil. If we ask him for a fish, he will not give us a serpent (Luke 11:11).

Of course, the Father is not the only member of the

three-in-one God. The perfect work of the sinless Son of God opened the door to the grace-saturated throne of our prayer-answering Father.

The Son Knows and Understands Our Weaknesses

Jesus Christ, fully God and fully man, is the one whose perfect life and sin-atoning death serves as the only possible bridge between sinful man and a holy God. Accordingly, all our prayers must go "through" him.

As Our Savior, Jesus Opened the Way to God

Our status as sinners originated when Adam and Eve rebelled against God in the Garden of Eden, resulting in enmity between them and God. As descendants of that first man and wife, we "all sinned" in Adam (Romans 5:12), inheriting the guilt of sin as well as a sin nature and consequent need for a Redeemer. The appearance of that Redeemer was foreshadowed right there in the garden.

Our sacrificial lamb. In an attempt to hide their shame by their own means, Adam and Eve sewed together a covering of fig leaves (Genesis 3:7-10). God saw that their sin and shame required a covering over; he also saw that their attempt was completely inadequate. So in mercy he provided a proper solution, foreshadowing the ultimate solution: God made them garments of animal skins (Genesis 3:21). The fact that these were skins speaks clearly of sin being so serious an affront against God's holy nature that it calls for death. Thus death entered the garden as a direct result of sin. Just as blood had to be shed to create adequate garments for Adam and Eve, thereby covering over the shame of sin, one day the blood of the Son, the Lamb of God (John 1:29), would be shed for sinful humanity, conclusively solving the problem of sin. The atoning work of Jesus on the cross, where he voluntarily offered his own shed blood, opened the way to God.

As Our High Priest, Jesus Stands Between Us and the Father

Now that Jesus has ascended back to the Father, his ministry to us continues. The door to God that the Son opened for us, through his death, he now keeps open in his role as our High Priest.

> Therefore, brothers, since we have confidence to enter the holy places by the blood of Jesus, by the new and living way that he opened for us through the curtain, that is, through his flesh, and since we have a great priest over the house of God, let us draw near with a true heart in full assurance of faith, with our hearts sprinkled clean from an evil conscience and our bodies washed with pure water. (Hebrews 10:19-22)

To its original Hebrew readers this passage carried far more meaning than it naturally does for us. "Holy places," "curtain," "great priest," "house of God," "draw near," "sprinkled clean," and "washed with pure water" all make reference to Old Testament physical practices that foreshadowed New Testament spiritual realities. In this complex, layered passage we see reference to Jesus as Savior ("the blood of Jesus") but also as our "great priest over the house of God."

Making a sacrificial offering. In ancient Israel the holy place was the exclusive, innermost room of the Temple in Jerusalem. It was open only to the high priest, only once per year, and only on the condition that he enter with the blood of an acceptable offering. As the ultimate High Priest, Jesus would later enter the *true* holy place in heaven, just once, to offer himself as the sinless sacrifice for his people (Hebrews 9:24-26; 10:1-14). By bringing his *own* blood to the throne of God, Jesus satisfied God's holy standard and bore away God's wrath against our sin (Romans 3:25). He achieved all of this "through his flesh," that is, by his humanity, the "curtain" torn apart to gain our access to God (Matthew 27:51).

Interceding. In addition to offering sacrifice while in the holy place, the high priest of ancient Israel would also pray for the people, interceding on their behalf before God. Again, this was ultimately a foreshadowing of Jesus. As our "great priest over the house of God," Jesus Christ is the eternal, living intercessor for God's household, the church, and is uniquely qualified for this role as the only one who has lived both in flesh as man and in heaven as God. This leads us to the next section.

As the God-Man, Jesus Understands Human Frailty

Just as the high priest in the Temple of ancient Israel could relate to and thus represent his people before God while in the physical holy of holies, our High Priest in the heavens took on flesh and lived on earth in that body for more than 30 years. Therefore, he can relate fully to our struggles.

> Since then we have a great high priest who has passed through the heavens, Jesus, the Son of God, let us hold fast our confession. For we do not have a high priest who is unable to sympathize with our weaknesses, but one who in every respect has been tempted as we are, yet without sin. Let us then with confidence draw near to the throne of grace, that we may receive mercy and find grace to help in time of need (Hebrews 4:14-16).

In interceding as High Priest on our behalf before the Father, Jesus therefore serves as our Mediator—one who stands in between God and man. He is the only one who can serve in this role.

In Jesus, every Christian possesses the acceptable Mediator who has already satisfied the holy wrath of God against our sin. As a result, we may boldly come to the Father "in Jesus' name"—that is, through the blood and complete worthiness of Jesus. But Jesus our great High Priest did more than complete a task *for* us; as our mediator he also *understands* us.

"In the days of his flesh, Jesus offered up prayers and supplications, with loud cries and tears, to him who was able to save him from death, and he was heard because of his reverence" (Hebrews 5:7). Are you not struck by the phrase "with loud cries and tears?" I am. The image of Jesus weeping should stamp upon our minds the reality of his humanity. When he cried out to the Father in anguish in the garden called Gethsemane—his raw emotions wrestling against the fact of his impending death—his bloody sweat was mingled with many tears. This helps us realize just how human Jesus was (and still is). Our theology rightly teaches us that Jesus is both 100% God and 100% man, but do we ponder enough the connection between the humanity of Jesus and the privilege of prayer?

It was in "the days of His flesh" that Jesus prayed. As the virgin-born Son of God, Jesus walked the same human road we walk (with the exception of the guilt of sin). As part of his humanity, the pattern he established at the beginning of his public ministry to rise early in the morning and go to a desolate place to pray continued until the night before his death (Mark 1:35; Matthew 26:36).

Through the disciplined lifestyle of prayer, Jesus admitted the weakness of his—and thus our—humanity. As Henry Thiessen puts it, "If the Son of God needed to pray, how much more do we need to wait upon God."[1] By calling us to pray, and by opening the door into this fellowship by means of the shed blood of his Son, God reminds us of our human weakness and invites us to ongoing fellowship in his presence.

From personal experience Jesus knows exactly how hard life can be in these bodies, having experienced every kind of temptation we will ever face. Our Savior is both sympathetic and empathetic. This is why we can confidently draw near to him in our time of need. His throne is truly a "throne of grace," dispensing mercy and help to us whenever we call upon God through him.

The Spirit Knows Our Groaning and Prays

In the process of prayer, the Holy Spirit plays a role both unique and unexpected.[2] Romans 8:26-27 puts it like this.

> Likewise the Spirit helps us in our weakness. For we do not know what to pray for as we ought, but the Spirit himself intercedes for us with groanings too deep for words. And he who searches hearts knows what is the mind of the Spirit, because the Spirit intercedes for the saints according to the will of God.

> Just as creation groans waiting for the fullness of redemption, and just as believers groan waiting for redemption from their earthly bodies (Romans 8:22-23), so the Holy Spirit groans in prayer! Three truths concerning the Spirit's ministry of prayer for us are here to be uncovered.

The Spirit Prays for Us Because We Are Weak

The Spirit who resides within "helps" us. He comes to our aid, rescues us, makes our prayers acceptable to God the Father, and helps shoulder our heavy burden. This is the ongoing ministry of the Spirit in our "weakness," our human frailties.

It is important for us to recognize that physical, emotional, and spiritual weaknesses reveal human frailty, yet are not necessarily the result of sin. Jesus, the sinless Son of God, experienced human frailty—enabling him to "sympathize with our weaknesses"—yet he never sinned (Hebrews 4:14-15). The omniscient Holy Spirit knows our weaknesses as well. He is the "Spirit of adoption" whom we have received from God and "by whom we cry, 'Abba! Father!'" (Romans 8:15).

The Spirit Prays for Us Because We Are Ignorant

Often we "do not know what to pray for" (Romans 8: 26). Sometimes we are aware of our ignorance¸ like the disciples who asked, "Lord, teach us to pray" (Luke 11:1). But often we are blind to it, like the sons of Zebedee who came to Jesus with their mother to demand a position of leadership—in response Jesus said, "You do not know what you are asking. Are you able to drink the cup that I am to drink?" (Matthew 20:22).

The Spirit prays for us because our knowledge is incomplete. Matthew Henry writes, "We are short-sighted … like foolish children, that are ready to cry for fruit before it is ripe and fit for them."[3] One of my young daughters loves to eat pears, but she does not know how to tell when they are ripe. As a result she will often grab a hard, green pear off the kitchen counter, take one bite, and leave the rest behind claiming "it is too hard." We often do the same. We want the fruit God is preparing for our future, but we want it *now*, before it is ripe. We do this because we are ignorant of what is best for us, and therefore don't know how to pray as we should. But the Spirit prays according to perfect knowledge. He prays with "groanings too deep for words." The Spirit pleads on our behalf in longings that are verbally inexpressible. This is his silent prayer ministry.

The Spirit Prays for Us Because God's Knowledge is Perfect

Paul continues in Romans 8:27, "He who searches hearts knows what is the mind of the Spirit." The omniscient Father always knows what the Spirit is thinking. So the Spirit's prayers include groanings that literally cannot be expressed in words, but at the same time the Father knows and understands the thoughts of the Spirit without the need for words. The Spirit of God knows the thoughts of God (1 Corinthians 2:11), and the Father knows the thoughts of the Spirit. The two are always in full agreement.

What then is the role of words in prayer? The same as the role of words in human communication generally. We do not have God's unlimited intellect, so we generally need words to help us capture thoughts in a more tangible form. Most of the time we also need words to communicate reasonably well with one another and with ourselves. This is why the Bible has come to us as it has—the Spirit "translating" God's thoughts to us in the form of words (1 Corinthians 2:13, 2 Peter 1:21).

Knowing that God's thoughts have been revealed to us by the Spirit in the written Word of God, we can have great confidence that the words the Spirit prays on our behalf to the Father are always perfectly in accord with Scripture. The same cannot be said of our own prayers, as R. C. Sproul admonishes,

> Professing Christians often ask God to bless or sanction their sin. They are even capable of telling their friends they have prayed about a certain matter and God has given them peace, despite what they prayed for was contrary to His will. Such prayers are thinly veiled acts of blasphemy, and we add insult to God when we dare to announce that his Spirit has sanctioned our sin by giving us peace in our souls. Such a peace is a carnal peace and has nothing to do with the peace that passes understanding, the peace that the Spirit is pleased to grant to those who love God and love his law.[4]

It should come as no surprise that sinful, rebellious people are capable of sinful, rebellious prayers. We can pray with our mouths, "*Thy* will be done," but mean in our hearts, "*My* will be done." This is where the Spirit helps us immensely. Galatians 4:6 says, "God has sent *the Spirit of his Son* into our hearts." The Holy Spirit *is* the Spirit of Jesus. The Spirit and the Son make our prayers acceptable to the Father according to his will. In other words, we pray, then on the basis of those prayers the Son and Spirit pray *for us* to the Father *on our behalf* in perfect accordance with the Father's will.

Jesus is our substitute, our representative before the

Father, and only on the basis of his work on the cross can we ever come before God. The same is true of our prayers! Just as we are unfit to come before the Father on our own behalf, neither are our prayers! They must be sanctified and purified—"translated," so to speak—by the Spirit and Son before they can come before the Father. If no unholy person can come before God, then neither can any unholy prayers. This is what it means to say that the Spirit intercedes for us "according to the will of God."

Then Let Us Draw Near

The Hebrews 4 and Hebrews 10 passages quoted earlier in this chapter teach us so much about prayer and the amazing triune God who listens. All the more important, then, that we notice that both these passages from Hebrews follow the same structure: *since God did A, we should do B*. In each passage the phrase "let us" is the pivot point, the transition from teaching to application.

Since we have in Jesus:

- this sacrificial lamb,
- this high priest and mediator,
- this God-man who understands our weaknesses and frailties,
- this Spirit who prays for us according to the will of God,

then *let us* draw near and pray with confidence, firm in the faith that Jesus understands and that the Son and the Spirit will carry our prayers perfectly to the throne of our loving Father who delights to respond to our prayers by giving us exactly what we need.

Because Jesus in his role as High Priest presented his own sacrificial blood to the Father, we can draw near to God in prayer—joyfully certain that our sins have been acceptably atoned for and, consequently, that God's wrath against us has been satisfied. Indeed all who approach God by repentant faith in Christ as Savior may enter with assurance by this new and living way (Hebrews 10:20), on the merit of Jesus alone, our High Priest who "always lives to make intercession" for us (Hebrews 7:25).

Indeed, all three members of the Trinity know all there is to know about you and are actively involved in answering your prayers. The Father turns his ear toward you and listens because he cares for his children. The Son intercedes as your High Priest because he gave his lifeblood to redeem you and become the only gateway to the Father. The Spirit helps carry your burdens to God. When you do not know how to pray the Holy Spirit pleads with the Father for you according to his good and perfect will.

Yet that's not primarily why you picked up this book. It is good to be assured of the breathtaking work of the triune God on our behalf behind the scenes when we pray—it is the rock-solid foundation we need to build the rest of our thinking upon. But you are probably reading this book because you are just like me; even though you know this theology of God is true, sometimes your prayers still are not answered. The heavens become as brass.

What then? What are the reasons God's hearing seems impaired? Is there anything you can do to remedy the problem? Let's begin to go there now.

❖ ❖ ❖

HEAVENLY FATHER, I praise you for hearing my voice. Thank you for loving me, a rebellious sinner, and demonstrating that love by bending down to listen to my cries for help. Your tender compassion not only invites me to pour out my heart to you, but your unchanging character as the giver of all good gifts creates within me the godly desire to pray.

LORD JESUS, thank you for voluntarily offering your atoning blood on my behalf in obedience to the Father's will. Thank you for allowing men created by you to shed your blood on the altar of Calvary to satisfy the Father's righteous law and propitiate his just wrath against my sin. Thank you for being my completely human, and therefore totally understanding, High Priest who always lives to intercede for me.

HOLY SPIRIT, I praise you for silently praying for me when my faith is too feeble to even find a voice or I am too ignorant to even know what to say. Knower of the mind of God and therefore the will of the Father, I am confident that your prayers always reach heaven's throne. When you pray, the heavens can never be as brass.

Amen.

Two
THE FATHER'S CHASTENING LOVE

God cares for his redeemed children, provides open access to his throne of grace through the perfect work of his Son, and has given us the Holy Spirit as the all-knowing helper who intercedes for us. That's just the best news anyone could ever hear. But what are we to conclude from these truths with regard to prayer? If God is now our Father, Jesus is our Savior and brother, and the Spirit is our helper, will all our prayers be automatically granted? If our sins have been punished by God in Christ does that mean our actions cannot possibly harm our relationship with God?

Before we can examine the causes of unanswered prayer, we must first address these kinds of questions. And the only way to think about such questions in a way that is helpful and biblical is to keep in mind the difference between our *judicial standing* before God and our *familial relationship* to him.

Our Judge Is Also Our Father

In God's role as judge, every person stands before him as either guilty or innocent. Either we are guilty of our sin or we are innocent because Jesus bore that guilt for us. By definition, then, *judicial standing* is a static, settled matter. You are on one side of the fence or the other, with no nuances or shadings. As Christians we can be certain that before God the judge we are innocent. And not only are we innocent, but we have also been declared righteous and adopted into the family of God, and he is our Father.

Our *standing* before God as judge is simple and clear-cut, settled once and for all. *It is not influenced by our behavior* because Jesus took the punishment for all our guilt and sin on the cross. But our *relationship* to God as Father is alive, rich, nuanced, dynamic, and personal. Our behavior certainly *can* influence this relationship. Although God the Father will never disown or reject us as his children, our behavior can please or displease him in a thousand different ways.

To be on the wrong side of God as judge is to be headed for eternal punishment—absolute disaster. But to be on the wrong side of God as Father because our sin has displeased him *is not to be outside his love, care, and mercy in the slightest*. It may help to think about it like this:

- Judicial guilt flows from God's holiness and leads to punishment as an act of retribution.
- Fatherly displeasure flows from God's love and leads to correction as an act of kindness.

We let ourselves in for a lot of needless grief when we begin to confuse our *judicial standing before God* with our *familial relationship to God*. It's an easy mistake to make. Someone may well say, for example, "I know God is now my father through faith in Christ and I know he loves me, so if Jesus paid for my sins on the cross how can the Father ever be angry with me?" It is true that God is never angry with believers *in a judicial sense*, for our sins have already been judged when they were imputed to his Son. However, there are times our sin provokes God's fatherly discipline. Scripture is clear on these distinctions:

- When God as Judge looks at the guilty he does not correct, chasten, guide, or discipline—he *punishes.*
- God as Father never looks at us as guilty, only as beloved children who are being foolish or wayward or even rebellious and insolent. Our sin grieves him, but it does not provoke vengeance, and he will never punish his children—instead he *corrects*, *chastens*, *guides*, *and disciplines* in order to get us back on the right path.

Justified Before the Judge

The instant you repented and believed in the Lord Jesus Christ as your Savior a great exchange took place. By faith you traded your sin for his righteousness. That is what 2 Corinthians 5:21 means when it says, "For our sake he made him to be sin who knew no sin, so that in him we might become the righteousness of God." While on the cross, Jesus willingly accepted the Father's placement of your sin's guilt and penalty upon him—your sins were *imputed* to him, meaning he was judged as if he were the guilty one. This is what Paul means when he says that the Father "made [the Son] to be sin." Peter says, "For Christ also suffered once for sins, the righteous for the unrighteous, that he might bring us to God" (1 Peter 3:18). He did this so that the moment we turn to God in faith, embracing Jesus as our sin-bearing Savior, the Son's righteousness is credited to us. If this is true of you, then you are now considered righteous by God and treated as such. Your judicial standing before God is a settled matter—you are justified and therefore counted as righteous forever. God views you not as one clothed in your own garments, which are filthy and stained by sin, but in the pure white garments of Jesus. That is what the apostle means when he declares that we have "become the righteousness of God" in Jesus.

Since the basis of our standing before God is Christ's righteousness, not our own, sin no longer affects our justification—our judicial standing—before God. We are fully accepted by him. We are continually loved by him. Romans 5:1 assures us, "Therefore, since we have been justified by faith [past tense], we have peace with God through our Lord Jesus Christ [present tense]." Romans 8:1 concludes, "There is therefore now no condemnation for those who are in Christ Jesus." Nothing can ever change that.

Children Before the Father

However, though our sin does not change the reality of our newfound relationship with God, it does impact our father/son or father/daughter relationship with him. God no longer deals with us as his enemies because by faith in Christ we have become his children, the siblings of Jesus (Hebrews 2:11) as well as his friends (John 15:15). God now deals with us as sons (Hebrews 12:7), which means he loves us too much to leave us alone in our sin. Though our "at peace" standing with God as our Judge is unchanging, our peaceful fellowship with him as our Father is affected when we disobey. This is because of his loyal love. He loves us too much to sit back and do nothing when sin threatens to harm us. The clearest passage where this is taught is Hebrews 12:4-11.

> In your struggle against sin you have not yet resisted to the point of shedding your blood. And have you forgotten the exhortation that addresses you as sons? "My son, do not regard lightly the discipline of the Lord, nor be weary when reproved by him. For the Lord disciplines the one he loves, and chastises every son whom he receives." It is for discipline that you have to endure. God is treating you as sons. For what son is there whom his father does not discipline? If you are left without discipline, in which all have participated, then you are illegitimate children and not sons. Besides this, we have had earthly fathers who disciplined us and we respected them. Shall we not much more be subject to the Father of spirits and live? For they disciplined us for a short time as it seemed best to them, but he disciplines us for our good, that we may share his holiness. For the moment all disci-

pline seems painful rather than pleasant, but later it yields the peaceful fruit of righteousness to those who have been trained by it.

When God the Father chastens his children the goal is always restorative—never punitive. To say it again, *God does not punish his children—he disciplines them*. There is an enormous difference.

- Punishment casts away; discipline restores.
- Punishment is for subjects of wrath; discipline is for the children of God.
- Punishment requires payment for sin; discipline corrects to protect and bless because sin has already been paid for by Jesus.
- Punishment focuses on past sins; discipline, while still dealing with sin, looks to the future blessing of obedience which follows true repentance.

The discipline of God is an evidence of his love, not hatred. If God does not discipline you when you go astray "then you are illegitimate children and not sons" (v 8). Therefore, do not be made anxious by the *presence* of discipline in your life. Be frightened by its *absence*. God disciplines those whom he loves. It is proof of your relationship. God does this so that you "may share his holiness" (v 10) and be "trained by it" in order that your life may yield "the peaceful fruit of righteousness" (v 11). As believers, God relates to us no longer as judge, but as Father.

So, how does God discipline us? One way is by withholding answers to prayer. Indeed, recognizing the validity of fatherly displeasure and our ongoing need for correction is key to understanding the issues surrounding unanswered prayer.

Prayer and Practical Holiness

God our Father cares far more about our holiness than anything else in our lives. His purpose in the earth is to save the lost and then increasingly conform the saved into the image of Jesus. Imagine if, as Christians, we were to get whatever we prayed for even when our lives were characterized by habitual sin? What incentive would we ever have to change? We would be like foolish children whose parents indulge their every whim and never require them to grow up.

When we sin, our Father is displeased. He wants us to flourish in Christ, but he knows that our sin only harms us. This explains why we see so clearly in Scripture a cause and effect relationship between the lack of practical righteousness (the living out of our positional righteousness in Christ) and unanswered prayer. When our life before God the Father does not line up with our standing before God the judge, we displease God and hinder our own prayers. Here are just a few supporting passages.

Old Testament

<u>Proverbs 15:29</u> "The LORD is far from the wicked, but he hears the prayer of the righteous." The "wicked" in this verse refers to the unbeliever, while the "righteous" is

the believer. The outworking of the believer's righteous *standing* before God is a growing, *practical* righteousness which results in the attentive opening of God's ears to his or her prayers.

Proverbs 28:9 "If one turns away his ear from hearing the law, even his prayer is an abomination." In other words, God hates the prayers of the person who deliberately rejects the Word of God, as opposed to the one who is merely ignorant of the truth. A very important question for every person to ask is, "What is the general posture of my heart toward the Word of God?" The warning here is serious. If you become calloused or "get your back up" in response to God's commands, then your prayers will be influenced negatively. But when your heart's response to the Word of God is humble and teachable then he delights to listen to your prayers.

Psalm 109:7 "When [the wicked man] is tried, let him come forth guilty; let his prayer be counted as sin!" This seems to describe an extreme state of wickedness. Though God is full of mercy, grace, and patience toward sinners, he remains holy and just at all times. Therefore, there is a point—known only to God—at which his tolerance with sin runs out and even a man's prayer becomes sin. For example, it is written of Esau that he reached the point where he could no longer find repentance, "though he sought it with tears" (Hebrews 12:17).

Isaiah 1:15-17 "When you spread out your hands, I will hide my eyes from you; even though you make many prayers, I will not listen; your hands are full of blood. Wash yourselves; make yourselves clean; remove the evil of your deeds from before my eyes; cease to do evil, learn to do good; seek justice, correct oppression; bring justice to the fatherless, plead the widow's cause." In this case, the leaders of Judah had become so wicked that God likened them to those of Sodom and Gomorrah. Perhaps they thought the consistency of their religious rituals got them a "pass" for sin and its judgment. But no, their religion was repulsive to God. "Your new moons and your appointed feasts my soul hates; they have become a burden to me; I am weary of bearing them" (Isaiah 1:14). Therefore, he called them to repentance, saying, in effect, "Until you turn away from your wickedness, even the multiplication of your prayers will not move me."

Was this just an Old Testament problem? Is the God of the New Testament so full of grace, love, mercy, and acceptance that he will always honor the prayers of his children? Clearly, this is not the case.

New Testament

James 4:3-4 "You ask and do not receive, because you ask wrongly, to spend it on your passions. You adulterous people! Do you not know that friendship with the world is enmity with God?" Here James reveals our natural tendency to pursue the fulfillment of our passions independently of God. Hiebert says of those to whom James wrote and, therefore, also of us,

> Instead of turning to God as the giver of every good and perfect gift (James 1:17), they attempt to satisfy their gnawing wants through their own efforts. Their

approach is self-centered and worldly. Instead of wrestling with God in prayer, they wrangle bitterly with men.[5]

Since not all desires are evil, it is legitimate for us to pray to God regarding them. However, good desires become evil when we seek to satisfy them in a fleshly manner, apart from pursuing God's will. As a result, we "do not receive" because we "ask wrongly" with self-centered motives for the building of our own little kingdoms where we are the ones who sit on the throne. Instead, Jesus teaches us to pray with God's agenda in mind, to "seek first the kingdom of God and his righteousness" (Matthew 6:33).

James 5:16 "Therefore, confess your sins to one another and pray for one another, that you may be healed. The prayer of a righteous person has great power as it is working." The prayers of the righteous person unleash "great power." The righteous person mentioned here is not the man who never sins (since there are no such people), but the man who, when he has sinned, honestly and humbly deals with it. He confesses his sin to God, and when necessary to others. When this kind of person prays, he is like Elijah, "a man with a nature like ours," but who brought about mighty acts of God by means of prayer that flowed from a heart of integrity (James 5:17-18).

John 14:13-15 "Whatever you ask in my name, this I will do, that the Father may be glorified in the Son. If you ask me anything in my name, I will do it. 'If you love me, you will keep my commandments.'" There is a great promise from the Lord here. By the enabling power of the Holy Spirit whom he would send, the resurrected and ascended Jesus would do "greater works" after returning to the Father (v 12). These God-glorifying works are considered greater than his pre-resurrection miracles because they are done through human beings—believers—and apart from the self-imposed limitations of Jesus' own humanity. Examples of these "greater works" are witnessed in the book of Acts. The gospel, "the power of God for salvation to everyone who believes," spread throughout the world as the direct result of prayer (Romans 1:16; Acts 4:31).

Two Conditions for Answered Prayer

What then is the kind of prayer that God will honor? The answer involves our heart and how we actually live.

Our heart position. Jesus calls us to pray in his name, that is, recognizing him as the only way to God and approaching his throne in full agreement with his Word so that the Father "may be glorified in the Son." Praying in Jesus' name means coming to God by the authority of Jesus, not our own. We must remember that outside the privileges that accompany our union with Christ we have no right to ever approach the Father. Paul Miller illustrates this well when he writes,

> Deep down, we just don't believe God is as generous as he keeps saying he is. That's why Jesus added the fine print—"ask in my name." Let me explain what that means.

Imagine that your prayer is a poorly dressed beggar reeking of alcohol and body odor, stumbling toward the palace of the great king. You have become your prayer. As you shuffle toward the barred gate, the guards stiffen. Your smell has preceded you. You stammer out a message for the great king: "I want to see the king." Your words are barely intelligible, but you whisper one final word, "Jesus, I come in the name of Jesus."

At the name of Jesus, as if by magic, the palace comes alive. The guards snap to attention, bowing low in front of you. Lights come on, and the door flies open. You are ushered into the palace and down a long hallway into the throne room of the great king, who comes running to you and wraps you in his arms.

The name of Jesus gives my prayers royal access. They get through. Jesus isn't just the Savior of my soul. He's also the Savior of my prayers. My prayers come before the throne of God as the prayers of Jesus.

"Asking in Jesus' name" isn't another thing I have to get right so my prayers are perfect. It is one more gift of God because my prayers are so imperfect.[6]

When our hearts bow to the authority of Jesus, resting not in any merit of our own, we agree with Jesus and are therefore praying in his name. As a result he promises, "I will do it."

Our practical obedience. There is another condition given by Jesus however—our obedience, which serves as proof (primarily to us) of our love for God. "If you love me, you will keep my commandments" (John 14:15). Love between the disciple and the Lord Jesus is proven by obedience to his commands (John 14:21-23; 15:14; 1 John 5:3). If we adhere to God's Word it proves we love him and walk according to his name. If we do not walk in obedience, then our self-proclaimed love for Christ may not be genuine. At the very least, it is immature, incomplete, indicating that we need the purifying power of *unanswered* prayer. This same John counsels us in his first letter,

> Beloved, if our heart does not condemn us, we have confidence before God; and whatever we ask we receive from him, because we keep his commandments and do what pleases him. And this is his commandment, that we believe in the name of his Son Jesus Christ and love one another, just as he has commanded us. Whoever keeps his commandments abides in him, and he in them. And by this we know that he abides in us, by the Spirit whom he has given us (1 John 3:21-24).

When we walk in obedience to God's Word, then there is no legitimate reason for our hearts to condemn us.[7] But when our hearts rightly condemn us because of specific disobedience and our spirits grieve along with the Holy Spirit (Ephesians 4:30), we must continue to pursue God in two ways.

1. Repent and confess those sins to God as an act of obedience for those who walk in the light of God's truth. The call to "confess our sins," in 1 John 1:9, is in contrast to the unbeliever who is unwilling to admit sin (v 8). When we obey God in this manner we receive the continuing application of his forgiveness, which he already says we possess in Christ (1 John 2:12). For the genuine believer confession is more than words falling off lips, but is the ongoing practice of our new lifestyle of repentance.

2. Return to the original commandment we obeyed when we were initially saved, "This is his commandment, that we believe in the name of his Son Jesus Christ" (1 John 3:23). Each time we repent—by the honest admission of our sin—we return to the cross and empty tomb in a fresh way, leading us toward a greater level of appreciation for the salvation God has graciously provided in his Son. This deepens our worship of God, which overflows in authentic praise (Romans 7:22-25; 1 Corinthians 15:56-57).

If we are trusting in Jesus Christ as our sin-bearer then God has dealt rightly with our sins. Therefore we can be assured that we are in right standing with him. Returning to this gospel truth brings to our minds the assurance that only God's Word provides.

> And this is the testimony, that God gave us eternal life, and this life is in his Son. Whoever has the Son has life; whoever does not have the Son of God does not have

life. I write these things to you who believe in the name of the Son of God that you may know that you have eternal life. And this is the confidence that we have toward him, that *if we ask anything according to his will he hears us*. And if we know that he hears us in whatever we ask, we know that we have the requests that we have asked of him (1 John 5:11-15).

What a rich passage! To address the high spots as they pertain to this chapter:

- If we have the Son of God, we know the Father, and we have eternal life.
- When we pray according to God's will—equivalent to praying in Jesus' name—he hears us.
- If we know he hears us, we know we have our requests.

This promise should not only compel us never to give up on prayer, but also to deal readily with our sins so that God's restorative discipline—for our own good and God's glory—is not longer or more difficult than it needs to be.

❖ ❖ ❖

HEAVENLY FATHER, thank you for loving me enough to discipline me when I sin. Forgive me, for I often forget that your correction is proof of your love, and when I forget this my spirit chafes against your correction in arrogant pride. Help me to receive your chastening by submitting to it with joy, even though it is sorrowful.

LORD JESUS, I praise you for keeping the eyes of your heart focused on the joy set before you, which enabled you to endure the cross—my cross. Thank you for absorbing the fullness of the Father's righteous wrath against my sin when you willingly allowed it to be imputed to you in order that your perfect righteousness may be credited to me the moment I believed.

HOLY SPIRIT, thank you for your enabling power and your presence, which is both comforting and convicting. You are the comforter who speaks assurance to my doubting soul. You are the convicter who bothers my conscience when I sin. Help me to grieve over my sin as you do, to linger in sorrow over it long enough to move me to repentance, but not so long that I get lost in self-absorption and forget the sufficiency of the Savior.

Amen.

Part Two
REASONS GOD DOES NOT HEAR

Three
PET SINS

The Care and Feeding of Rebellion

We often like having animals as pets because we believe they can enrich our lives. We like attending to them, interacting with them, and just having them around. Strangely enough, it's almost exactly the same with pet sins.

Somehow we become aware of a particular kind of sin and feel drawn to it. Maybe we have noticed that other people who own the same pet sin seem to enjoy its presence in their lives. We begin to imagine that having the same sin come live with us would be enriching or thrilling or a nice distraction from the patterns and responsibilities of daily life. And in the process of self-seduction we lose sight of the fact that this pet is not in fact something positive or even neutral. It is sin, a complete and unqualified negative, and a lot more like a coiled rattlesnake than a playful puppy.

Yet we invite it in, and it begins to live with us. Maybe we even have to go to some considerable expense or effort to acquire or keep it, but that's okay, because we really want it around—at least some of the time. As we begin to feed it and groom it and play with it, it begins to integrate itself into our lives, and its presence comes to feel natural. But then one day it turns on us, or does something shocking or disgusting, and we recoil. Of course, we are only surprised because we have forgotten our pet's true nature. But now we are so accustomed to having it around that we don't think very seriously about getting rid of it. We return to caring for this pet sin, and after awhile the same thing happens. Once again we are shocked and repulsed, although maybe a little less than before. So we continue to keep it around; our pet sin is now part of us. We have come to cherish this addition to our lives, and it is actually difficult to imagine living without it.

The Bible offers a vivid picture of our perverse tendency to love the very thing that has harmed us. "Like a dog that returns to his vomit is a fool who repeats his folly" (Proverbs 26:11). This is exactly how we behave when we keep on indulging a pet sin even when we see how bad it can be for us. We return to the same sins repeatedly, gobbling them up greedily even though we know they make us sick.

We all have these particular areas of weakness—pet sins we are strangely attached to despite the pain and grief they have caused us. What is it that prevents us from seeing the awfulness of our sin? Forgive the graphic imagery (you can blame Solomon), but what keeps us from smelling and tasting the vomit?

Our fallen nature, which actively loves sin, blinds us to just how awful it really is. We fail to see that it brings us far more harm and pain than anything else. We fail to see it as so wicked that Jesus had to die for it. We fail to see how much it grieves the Holy Spirit. And we fail to see that every sin is a brazen act of rebellion against our loving Father.

Rebels with a Future

Beginning with the garden of Eden, man's main problem has always been a desire to be independent of God's rule. In effect, we want to dethrone him and take his place. Deep down our flesh does not want to be restrained by anyone, even God—*especially* God. This is our universal rebellion, the tragic reality underlying the relationship between man and God and our most deeply rooted problem.

This willfulness manifests itself at the heart level (Galatians 5:17). We often get sick of sin's guilt and consequences, and it makes us vomit. But then we turn around and do it all over again, continually proving that our nature is as senselessly defiant as the Bible says it is (Jeremiah 17:9).

But the good news is that God has promised to redeem a people for himself, purifying them and making them perfect in the Son. Therefore, if we are truly born of God, the indwelling Holy Spirit is ever at work in our hearts convicting us of our rebellion. When God the Father drew us to himself (John 6:44), we beheld the glory of Jesus in the gospel (2 Corinthians 3:18), and we were convicted, regenerated, and transformed by the Spirit (John 3:6; 16:8). Instantly our affections began to change, reflecting the beauty and newness of life in Christ instead of the stench and oldness of death (Ephesians 2:3,13).

This was not our work, but God's. It is only because of his regenerating and transforming work in us that we want anything to do with him and his will (Philippians 2:13). Our sin nature has no interest in holiness. Only the new heart that God gifted to us by the Holy Spirit is even capable of desiring to be like Jesus, who always did "the things that are pleasing to [the Father]" (John 8:29).

So when we allow that sin nature to rule us, when we turn back to the vomit like a dog that can't help himself, when we continue to cherish our pet sins even though we know they are disgusting—we still have a God who loves us too much to let us remain blind to our pitiful condition. God is committed to freeing us gradually and progressively from our sin, and the Father delights to bend down to listen to our voice. At the same time, if we will not pray honestly to God or obey him, he may take another approach. God our Father may go silent on us, withdrawing himself from our lives as much as is necessary to refocus our attention. He does this not out of punishment, but for chastening and discipline, so we may see the seriousness of our sin and begin to be filled with the godly grief that leads to true repentance (2 Corinthians 7:10).

Cherishing Pet Sins

One reason we might come under the chastening love of God arises from our natural inclination to rebel against God by cherishing sin. Psalm 66:16-20 says it plainly.

> Come and hear, all you who fear God, and I will tell what he has done for my soul. I cried to him with

my mouth, and high praise was on my tongue. *If I had cherished iniquity in my heart, the Lord would not have listened.* But truly God has listened; he has attended to the voice of my prayer. Blessed be God, because he has not rejected my prayer or removed his steadfast love from me!

"Come and hear" is the psalmist's invitation to fellow believers to observe the works of God in his life which occurred in answer to prayer. He wants us, the readers, to bless God as he does—to join him in "high praise," for "truly God has listened" to the voice of our prayer and "has not rejected [our] prayer or removed his steadfast love from [us]!"

Sandwiched between two powerful declarations of the faithfulness of God to answer prayer, however, is this sober warning: "If I had cherished iniquity in my heart, the Lord would not have listened." Cherished sin—pet sins—can be a cause of unanswered prayer.

To cherish sin is to *look forward to doing what God forbids*. It is the Old Testament equivalent of making "provision for the flesh, to gratify its desires" (Romans 13:14). It involves allowing certain thought patterns, habits of life, or questionable relationships to remain in order to provide opportunity for the satisfaction of fleshly pleasures. We could say it means our flesh prefers to keep a pet sin "on the side," just in case God's promise of something better does not pan out. In fact, the precise opposite is true: to the extent that we keep investing foolishly in satisfaction outside of God, we cannot and will not find the greater treasure that is to be found only in him. Can we not learn from Satan's tempting of Eve? It was as if he said to her, "Reach out, Eve. Take it, just in case that stingy God has hidden something good from you." And how did *that* turn out?

The "cherishing" of sin mentioned in Psalm 66 may even include "praying for God's help in order to be able to commit some form of sin."[8] Have you seen this potential in your own life? Our depraved hearts are so wicked that we can deceive ourselves into praying for something that enables our rebellion, even convincing ourselves that our sinful desire is God's good will for us.

Kill Your Pets

To address this persistent problem of our sinful flesh we must choose to follow the radical counsel of Jesus, viciously ridding our lives of anything that aids the fulfillment of our fleshly lusts.

> If your right eye causes you to sin, tear it out and throw it away. For it is better that you lose one of your members than that your whole body be thrown into hell. And if your right hand causes you to sin, cut it off and throw it away. For it is better that you lose one of your members than that your whole body go into hell. (Matthew 5:29-30)

If you are aware of your struggle to resist a particular form of temptation, then you must make no provision for it. Instead you must amputate from your life whatever triggers your temptations. To walk the edge of sin is a fool's game, for at any moment you could plunge yourself and your loved ones into an abyss of pain, grief, and tragedy. Instead you must stand firmly upon the granite cliff of steadfast obedience to God's Word.

To *establish*, *maintain*, or *permit* the existence in your life of any avenues by which your flesh could seek to fulfill its rebellious desires—this is the cherishing of pet sin. By this you will guarantee the short-circuiting of your prayers. This effort to live two different lives—one in which you cherish God and another in which you cherish sin—is *the very definition of being double-minded*. And as James, the brother of our Lord, put it so memorably when discussing prayer in times of trial, "that person must not suppose that he will receive anything from the Lord" (James 1:7).

God's Intentional Deafness

The deafness of God, of course, is intentional. Psalm 66 says that the Lord "would not" have listened, not that he could not. "Thus says the LORD who made the earth, the LORD who formed it to establish it—the LORD is his name: Call to me and I will answer you, and will tell you great and hidden things that you have not known" (Jeremiah 33:2-3). This specific promise to the prophet Jeremiah nevertheless contains truth for all time. God can and will, when he chooses, do great and mighty things in response to prayer. But when he refuses to answer our prayers it has nothing to do with his ability. He could always answer, but at times he chooses not to. And sometimes it is because we cherish sin.

In these seasons God closes his ears to our voice because he intends to open our eyes to sin that we need to turn from. Such deafness by God and silence from God can be brief or extended. It can be experienced as relatively minor or quite severe. This may leave us feeling numb in our souls, joyless in our hearts, and unstable in our faith. Indeed at times God's discipline may need to be more severe in order to create within us "a broken spirit; a broken and contrite heart" (Psalm 51:17). All of this is the loving, chastening discipline of a Father who loves us too much to let us be content in our sin.

Is there a particular pet sin that you have been unwilling to repent of? Is there a form of rebellion that you find even some small pleasure hanging on to? Why not confess it right now? Why not determine to immediately destroy every means, large or small, blatant or subtle, by which you make provision for it to remain present in your life? Why not do all in your power to open God's ears to your voice once again?

God Has Heard

As we return to where the psalmist began we see him end on a very encouraging note. "But truly God has listened; he has attended to the voice of my prayer. Blessed be God, because he has not rejected my prayer or removed his steadfast love from me!" (Psalm 66:19-20). When we deal honestly with our sin before our holy but forgiving God, we agree with the psalmist and share his renewed confidence in God's grace. God cares for us in our weakness. For our own good he graciously turns us away from cherishing sin. Even in this painful process of discipline he does not remove his steadfast love (grace) from us. In the midst of our chastening we are assured of his love and of the security that is ours in Christ. If we are truly born again, then nothing—not even our heart's lingering desire to cherish sin—can ever "separate us from the love of God in Christ Jesus our Lord" (Romans 8:39).

> *God rejects the prayers of those*
> *who cherish iniquity,*
> *but receives the prayers of those who battle sin.*

❖ ❖ ❖

HEAVENLY FATHER, I praise you for hearing my voice. I thank you that you love me enough to discipline me, to close your ears to my prayers in order that my eyes may be opened to my pet sins so that I see them for what they really are—displays of my independent, defiant nature that resists full submission to your good will. Thank you for opening my eyes to the inner workings of my heart and the presence of corrupt affections so that I may humbly confess my sins.

LORD JESUS, thank you for willingly offering your atoning blood on my behalf to be shed on the cross of Calvary as full payment for my rebellion against the Father's rightful authority and perfect will. Thank you for remaining faithful and righteous to forgive me and to cleanse me from all unrighteousness. I praise you that because of your resurrection and ascension to the Father's right hand, you are my ever-living High Priest who makes continual intercession for me.

HOLY SPIRIT, I praise you for your faithful, convicting work in my heart. Thank you for opening my spiritual eyes to see how often I delight in sin, even to the extent that I make provision for my flesh, sometimes convincing myself that my will is your will, and thereby rationalizing my actions and justifying my own rebellion. O, may you cultivate a deeper submission of my will to yours that I may walk daily in your sanctifying power, rather than the corrupting power of my flesh.

Amen.

Four
NEGLECTED DUTIES

When Conflicts and Offenses Go Unresolved

Some sins are more passive than active. We may call these sins of omission rather than sins of commission because they are all about what we *don't* do. These sins involve neglecting (and sometimes refusing) to do what is right rather than willfully doing what is plainly forbidden. In his Sermon on the Mount, Jesus gave pointed warnings against two such areas of neglect that are especially pertinent to this matter of unanswered prayer. Mishandling either area can severely damage not only our horizontal relationships with others, but also our familial relationship with the Father and consequently the effectiveness of our prayers. These two areas are the delay of conflict resolution and the withholding of forgiveness.

The Delay of Conflict Resolution

The Bible is clear. Each of us is a selfish sinner. No exceptions. Therefore, conflict is simply inevitable.

Conflict is more than simple disagreement. Peacemaker Ministries defines it as, "A difference in opinion or purpose that frustrates someone's goals or desires." In a conflict at least one of the people involved, if not both, becomes upset because he fears he may not get what he wants—even if what he wants is simply to have someone else see a particular situation the way he does. James strikes at the heart of it when he writes, "What causes quarrels and what causes fights among you? Is it not this, that your passions are at war within you?" (James 4:1).

Notice that James didn't say "sinful passions," for sometimes we get into conflicts over passions that are good and honorable. Moreover, people can sometimes deeply disagree over significant matters without an actual conflict arising. These distinctions only begin to hint at how complex this area can become. For our immediate purposes, however, it's enough to say that generally we recognize conflict when we're in it—we know the difference between simply disagreeing with someone and finding our hearts rising up in offense or frustration or anger because of something someone else does or says or believes.

As long as we live this side of heaven, we will continue to experience conflicts with others, and we will continue to hear God's call to repentance and greater growth in the midst of conflict. Relational conflict, like everything else God puts in our path, is used by him for our good. When responded to with humility, long-suffering, grace, and forgiveness, such conflict leads to stronger, more Christ-honoring relationships. The transformative grace of God converts that which would weaken human relationships into something that substantially strengthens them—evil is turned into good, and cursing into blessing. This makes us more like Jesus and equips us to be better testimonies to the redemptive power of God in a world that is desperate for grace and peace.

Indeed, how we handle conflict reveals our heart's true relationship to the gospel. Whether we are the offender or the offended, if we choose to delay the resolving of our conflicts with one another then we short-change ourselves—hindering our own spiritual growth and that of others. To resist or neglect the resolution of conflict, especially between yourself and another Christian, is a small but real rejection of the gospel itself. No wonder it can hinder our prayers.

So, what do we do about it?

Have a Sense of Urgency

The Bible exhorts us to do everything in our power to resolve conflict ASAP. The clearest scriptural call to this duty is found in Matthew 5:23-24, "So if you are offering your gift at the altar and there remember that your brother has something against you, leave your gift there before the altar and go. First be reconciled to your brother, and then come and offer your gift."

Those are radical words. The original Jewish hearers were able to place these words of Jesus into a familiar context. For them, the Lord was referring to animal sacrifice within the Temple. This was a solemn, somber, and deeply meaningful act of worship and trust that lay at the heart of the Old Covenant. For us, this would correspond to our most significant interactions with God as his children, including private worship through personal prayer as well as corporate worship. But here Jesus is saying there is one good reason to stop right in the middle of it all—because you have other, more important business.

Jesus considers conflict resolution among believers a higher priority than our worship of God himself! He tells us plainly that it is better to interrupt or postpone our worship than to engage in it under the wrong conditions. This passage does not explicitly say that unresolved conflict is a cause for unanswered prayer. But it does say that *God is not interested in receiving our worship until we honestly face the wrongs we have committed against one another*. While it is possible to argue distinctions between those two, they are distinctions without any real difference. To come before God aware of unresolved conflict with another Christian, when it is within our power to seek resolution to that conflict, renders our worship false and hypocritical. Unresolved conflict hinders our relationship with God, and this hinders our prayers.

As if this were not sufficient cause to pursue reconciliation with fellow believers whenever we become aware of unresolved conflict, here are five more reasons.

1. **Delaying conflict resolution opens the door to Satan's destructive work.** "Be angry and do not sin; do not let the sun go down on your anger, and give no opportunity to the devil" (Ephesians 4:26-27).

2. **Delaying conflict resolution evidences a lack of brotherly love and concern.** "If your brother sins against you, go and tell him his fault, between you and him alone. If he listens to you, you have gained your brother" (Matthew 18:15). "Brothers, if anyone is caught in any transgression, you who are spiritual should restore him in a spirit of gentleness. Keep watch on yourself, lest you too be tempted" (Galatians 6:1).

3. **Delaying conflict resolution harms yourself and others.** "But if you bite and devour one another, watch out that you are not consumed by one another" (Galatians 5:15).

4. **Delaying conflict resolution often fuels greater strife, a fruit of the flesh.** "Now the works of the flesh are evident … enmity, strife, jealousy, fits of anger, rivalries, dissensions, divisions" (Galatians 5:19-20).

5. **Delaying conflict resolution may provoke severe discipline from God.** "I do not commend you … in the first place, when you come together as a church, I hear that there are divisions among you. … Anyone who eats and drinks without discerning the body eats and drinks judgment on himself. That is why many of you are weak and ill, and some have died. … But when we are judged by the Lord, we are disciplined" (1 Corinthians 11:17-18, 29-32).

Aim for Restoration

Instead of avoiding our interpersonal conflicts or delaying their resolution, Scripture compels us to pursue peace relentlessly. Notice the active verbs in the following verses that urge us to pursue and preserve godly personal relationships.

> *Come to terms quickly* with your accuser (Matthew 5:25).

> So then let us *pursue what makes for peace* and for mutual upbuilding (Romans 14:19).

> *Aim for restoration*, *comfort* one another, *agree* with one another, *live in peace*; and the God of love and peace will be with you (2 Corinthians 13:11).

> So *flee* youthful passions and *pursue* righteousness, faith, love, and peace, *along with those* who call on the Lord from a pure heart (2 Timothy 2:22).

> *Strive for peace* with everyone, and for the holiness without which no one will see the Lord (Hebrews 12:14).

> Let him *turn away* from evil and *do good*; let him *seek peace and pursue it* (1 Peter 3:11).

So we see that conflict often goes unresolved because we allow it—we neglect to take conflict as seriously as Scripture implores and commands us to. Another closely related reason is that we neglect to forgive one another from the heart—again, because we refuse to or simply because we don't know how. This, too, can hinder our prayers.

The Withholding of Forgiveness

The New Testament contains a number of passages that many of us would prefer weren't there. I'm thinking in particular of those verses that shake up our convenient theology by reminding us that God's holiness makes serious demands—even upon those whom God has adopted as his beloved children. Especially for those of us who celebrate the doctrines of grace, it can be a wake-up call, for example, to realize that the New Testament expects us to extend to those who sin against us the same level of free and unqualified forgiveness that God has extended to us. Indeed, the Bible permits no other standard.

> Be kind to one another, tenderhearted, forgiving one another, *as God in Christ forgave you* (Ephesians 4:32).

> Put on then, as God's chosen ones, holy and beloved, compassion, kindness, humility, meekness, and patience, bearing with one another and, if one has a complaint against another, forgiving each other; *as the Lord has forgiven you*, so you also must forgive (Colossians 3:12-13).

These passages appear in Paul's letters, written some years after the victorious resurrection of Christ from the dead. But prior to the cross, where sin was once and for all defeated, Jesus sounded an even more sobering note.

Hardly a more serious warning to any believer exists than this found near the end of Jesus' teaching on prayer. "For if you forgive others their trespasses, your heavenly Father will also forgive you, but if you do not forgive others their trespasses, neither will your Father forgive your trespasses" (Matthew 6:14-15).

Jesus' reference to God as "your Father" indicates that he intended this warning for genuine Christians. As Christians, we repent of our sins in part by praying to God and asking for forgiveness. Yet the very Son of God, whose death made our forgiveness possible, here tells us that if we refuse to forgive others then God will turn a deaf ear to our own confessions of sin. The message is plain. The Christian who refuses to refuses to release another from the debt of sin will face divine consequences.

The way of forgiveness. Since self-centered pride is the heart problem behind an unforgiving spirit, the remedy is humility and others-focused love. We need to humble ourselves before those whom we have wronged as well as those who have wronged us. We must clothe ourselves "with humility toward one another, for 'God opposes the proud but gives grace to the humble'" (1 Peter 5:5). When we love God enough to obey his command to forgive others as we have been forgiven (Ephesians 4:32; Colossians 3:13), and when we love others enough to release them from their sin debt (1 Corinthians 13:5), this dissolves our pride and sets us free from the prison of fear. "There is no fear in love, but perfect love casts out fear" (1 John 4:18).

Whenever we are sinned against we must choose to remember the extent to which God has released us from

our sins through the blood of his Son (Revelation 1:5).
In addition, we must bring to mind the wealth of "every
spiritual blessing" he has showered upon us in Christ
Jesus (Ephesians 1:3). This will compel us to guard our
hearts against a bitter, vengeful spirit, as Peter exhorts,
"Finally, all of you, have unity of mind, sympathy,
brotherly love, a tender heart, and a humble mind. Do
not repay evil for evil or reviling for reviling, but on the
contrary, bless, for to this you were called, that you may
obtain a blessing" (1 Peter 3:8-9).

For your consideration. A pattern of refusal to
forgive others reveals a lack of understanding or appreciation of the long-suffering of God. There are two possible
reasons for this: Christian immaturity and rebellion, or
something much more dire.

Because forgiveness does not come naturally to man,
forgiving others is an evidence of God's grace being active
in one's life. The flip side of this is that a consistent lack of
forgiveness may be an indication that we have never experienced the saving grace of God. Therefore you and I must
consider this: *the harder it is for us to genuinely forgive others,
the more likely we have not in fact been forgiven by God.* If
we habitually hold grudges against others who hurt us, then
God's warning is very strong, "For judgment is without
mercy to one who has shown no mercy" (James 2:13).

A consistent refusal to forgive, *as God has forgiven*,
calls into question the genuineness of the professing
Christian's conversion. The Spirit calls you to examine
yourself, "to see whether you are in the faith. Test
[yourself]" (2 Corinthians 13:5).

The Underlying Theology

Why does the Bible put all this emphasis on conflict resolution? Underlying all the reasons we've already discussed, there is a theological reason. The Scriptural call to reconciliation among brothers and sisters in Christ grows from a deeply important gospel-motivated root. In Christ, God "reconciled us to himself and gave us the ministry of reconciliation" (2 Corinthians 5:18).

This ministry of reconciliation involves announcing the gospel, the message of reconciliation, to unbelievers who need to place their hope and trust in Christ. But it also includes the practice of Christians being reconciled to one another (glance back at the Scriptures cited earlier in the Aim for Restoration section, for example). In the richness of his grace, God uses conflict in our lives to drive us continually back to the cross of Jesus where we see that our sins were paid for and where the ultimate reconciliation (of sinners to God) was accomplished. This "gospel focus" once again propels us toward the obedience of pursuing reconciliation with our siblings in the family of God.

As you read this chapter, is your soul grieved by some unresolved offense in your own life? Is there a brother or sister in Christ whom you have sinned against, or who has sinned against you? If so, here are the key issues.

Inadequate effort. Have you made every attempt to seek out him or her, preferably face-to-face? If not, then let the pressing words of Jesus move you toward obedience.

Uncooperative response. Have you sought such

forgiveness but he or she will not grant it, or will not meet with you? In this case, you do not need to abstain from participation in public worship or private prayer. If you have obeyed Romans 12:18 ("so far as it depends on you, live peaceably with all"), then you must pray and wait, and wait and pray. Continue to ask, "Lord, search me. Change me. Show me if there is one more right thing I must do." Continue to pray for the Holy Spirit to choreograph a grace-filled reconciliation. And through it all guard your heart from bitterness, wrath, and an unforgiving spirit (Ephesians 4:31-32). "Aim for restoration" (2 Corinthians 13:11). Such is the life of a true Christian.

It is time to view passive rebellion as seriously as God does. "So whoever knows the right thing to do and fails to do it, for him it is sin" (James 4:17). God will not sit idle if we neglect biblical duties that impose specific responsibilities upon us. Instead, by the means of unanswered prayer, he will allow us to feel acutely that our fellowship with him has been hindered. Our heavenly Father desires to be worshiped "in spirit and truth" (John 4:23), and he loves his children too much to allow us to be left in harm's way through ongoing unforgiveness.

Genuine Christians are forgiven sinners who live in community with other forgiven sinners, all of whom realize that until the end of their earthly lives there will be a need to regularly grant and receive forgiveness. When you live with this mindset you can be assured that the often-neglected duty to resolve conflict will not hinder the effectiveness of your own prayer life.

*God rejects the prayers of those
who actively harbor offenses,
but receives the prayers of those
who seek peace and pursue it.*

❖ ❖ ❖

HEAVENLY FATHER, *thank you for opening my spiritual ears to hear your Word, and the eyes of my heart to see ways in which I rebel against you passively, by neglecting to do as you have commanded. Forgive me for my carelessness, laziness, and willfulness. Make my heart soft and submissive, like pliable clay in the potter's hands.*

LORD JESUS, *you taught, "Blessed are the peacemakers." I praise you for being my peacemaker, for reconciling me—a wayward sinner—back to my loving heavenly Father. Indeed, you are the Good Shepherd who has led me to the heavenly pasture; you are the guardian of my soul. Make me eternally grateful for your blood that was shed to purchase my redemption. Let me never forget the price you paid to make my forgiveness not only possible, but also real.*

PERSISTENT SPIRIT, *guard my heart from the slow-growing callous that leaves it dull to hearing, and feeling-less in regard to the biblical urgency to resolve my conflicts. Stand as an armed soldier at the door of my heart forbidding bitterness from taking up residence as the result of lingering anger or the stubborn refusal to forgive those who wrong me. Show me how I have grieved you and quenched your powerful work in my heart, and move my will to repent.*

Amen.

Five
RELIGIOUS SINS
The Trap of Self-Worth

So far we have looked at how our prayers can be hindered by sins that are fairly obvious: the care and feeding of pet sins and the neglect of duties clearly required of us by Scripture. This chapter addresses a variety of sin that is perhaps less obvious but even more damaging to our souls and crippling to our prayers—our religious sins.

Hiding beneath the cloak of our perceived goodness, religious sins are those that feed self-awareness of our spirituality. Instead of driving us to God in humble dependence upon his grace, they blind us, fuel self-righteousness, breed spiritual apathy, and often neutralize the Holy Spirit's conviction. Religious sins are hazardous because they produce false confidence in the soul. In a vicious cycle of increasing self-worship, they steadily feed the pride from which they were born. This impels us to strive for godliness in the flesh, the deep irony being that the more we do this the less godly we become. Striving in the flesh only enslaves us further to the law's conditional approval and its resulting condemnation, and increasingly cuts us off from the grace of God that is our only source of hope.

Under the influence of religious sins we become dangerously pleased with our own spiritual performance and become judgmental of others in our perceived superiority. This ultimately results in conflict with God, for "God opposes the proud, but gives grace to the humble" (James 4:6). Religious sins can provide us with an outward appearance of loving God, even as they cripple our capacity to truly be changed by transforming grace.

What is the solution? How do we escape from this cycle of self-congratulation and self-elevation? Just as you and I would never have conceived of the atoning death and resurrection of the Son of God as the answer to sin, the answer to this question is likewise one we would never have chosen ourselves.

We generally escape from the vicious cycle of religious sins only when God spiritually breaks us.

Spiritual Pride and the Blessing of Brokenness

Returning again to the Sermon on the Mount from Matthew 5—a discourse that pointedly and repeatedly confronts spiritual pride—it is intriguing to see that Jesus begins with the blessing of brokenness.

- It is the poor in spirit who will receive kingdom riches, not those who feel spiritually wealthy in themselves (v 3).
- It is those who mourn who will be comforted, not those who are oblivious to their own sinfulness (v 4).
- It is those who crave righteousness who will know the satisfaction of a righteousness gifted to them (v 6).

Jesus has our attention. In a world of so much pain and suffering and frustration and evil there *are* some who will be comforted and satisfied. How do we become the people of whom the Lord speaks here? He does not yet tell us, at least not directly. Moments later in the same discourse, however, Jesus sets out for us in the starkest terms just how desperately we need new hearts. Exposing us all for the fallen creatures we are, he reveals that:

- The true heart of murder is found in common, everyday anger (vv 21-22).
- The true heart of adultery is found in that initial lustful thought (vv 27-28).
- The true heart of wicked vengeance is found in our daily failures to respond to others in love and humility (vv 38-47).

From there, in Matthew 6, Jesus moves quickly to the subject of this chapter: religious sins.

The Pharisees—the hypocrites of Jesus' day—were preoccupied with displaying their righteousness. They sought to impress others with their supposed spiritual maturity because they were impressed with it themselves. Such hypocrisy was a frequent subject for Jesus, for he knew that even those who would be filled with his Holy Spirit following his resurrection would continue to struggle with this religious sin. In the parable of the Pharisee and the tax collector at prayer, we find an especially helpful lesson in the delusions of self-worth.

> Two men went up into the temple to pray, one a
> Pharisee and the other a tax collector. The Pharisee,
> standing by himself, prayed thus: 'God, I thank you
> that I am not like other men, extortioners, unjust,
> adulterers, or even like this tax collector. I fast twice a
> week; I give tithes of all that I get.' But the tax collector,
> standing far off, would not even lift up his eyes to
> heaven, but beat his breast, saying, 'God, be merciful
> to me, a sinner!' I tell you, this man went down to his
> house justified, rather than the other. For everyone
> who exalts himself will be humbled, but the one who
> humbles himself will be exalted (Luke 18:10-14).

The Pharisee confidently justified himself, believing
he had no need of God's mercy. The Pharisee was self-
righteous. His confidence was built on the great, awful
lie that the righteousness which saves is found *within* the
good or religious person. But the tax collector humbly
offered to God his truckload of sin as he pleaded for
mercy. He was just an average sinner, and well aware that
righteousness could only come to him as a gift. If he was
ever to be justified, God would have to do it. He realized
that the only way anyone can ever be in good standing
with God is if God counts the righteousness of Jesus to
the credit of the sinner. Theologians call this imputation.
Righteousness can only be ours if God *imputes* the righteousness of Christ to us.

In this parable both men went to the temple to pray,
but God only listened to one of them. The tax collector
brought to God humility of faith birthed in brokenness,

and he was heard and justified by God. But the Pharisee, while outwardly religious in many of the right ways, brought to God only an arrogant sense of superiority and confidence in his own flesh. The most meaningful difference between these two men was their hearts, not their behavior. The tax collector was a broken man who saw himself with a certain humble clarity. The Pharisee, full of religious sins, was blinded by the curse of self-honor.

To be sure, the Bible never teaches that outward manifestations of an inner righteousness are wrong in themselves. There *is* an outward righteousness that is legitimately connected to the true inner righteousness of Christ imputed to us by the Father. Jesus even says later in the Sermon on the Mount that outward manifestations can serve as proof of inner righteousness (Matthew 7:18-20). But there is also an *apparent* outward righteousness that is connected to nothing except its own sense of self-importance. It is the righteousness of independence and self-justification, a false righteousness that presumes to possess an inherent, self-contained goodness— something only God possesses in and of himself.

The challenge we all face is that we tend to start congratulating ourselves. We place our confidence in our performance (our practical righteousness) rather than the righteousness of Christ that has been imputed to us (our actual righteousness).

So when Jesus warned, "Beware of practicing your righteousness before other people," he was not diminishing the importance of practical righteousness or forbidding its outward display. The focus in that warning is on the Pharisaical quest for self-honor, the religious hypocrites' motive "to be seen by [others]" as especially holy (Matthew 6:1). The Pharisees' problem was not their practice of religion. It was not that they gave alms, or prayed, or fasted in public settings. It was that they did these things in public with a particular motivation—to draw attention to themselves so that people might think better of them (see Matthew 6:2,5,16). The best that such vain striving for approval can ever attain is the shallow, fleeting, and ultimately meaningless approval of man. It fails completely to achieve the eternal, glorious approval of God himself.

This parable of the Pharisee and the tax collector provides us another clear category for unanswered prayer: God rejects the prayers of the self-satisfied and the self-righteous, but accepts the prayers of the humble and broken.

In Tom Hovestol's book, *Extreme Righteousness: Seeing Ourselves in the Pharisees,* he calls the Pharisees "scoundrels" and the "best supporting actors" of the Gospel accounts. Hovestol indicts every one of us as a Pharisee, warning us of the self-righteousness that lurks within.

> Pharisaism's fatal flaw is self-righteousness. It lurks just beneath the surface of our evangelical souls. But we do not see it! Why? Perhaps we live such good lives that we look for sin in all the wrong places! We tune in to the external symbols of goodness but miss the internal symptoms of evil. Jesus does not want us, however, to live our lives in the pseudo-security

of human righteousness. While on earth, He loved people too much to permit them to continue their merry religious ways blinded to their true spiritual condition. Instead he regularly engaged in the ministry of enabling religious people to find freedom and true life.[9]

To help you and I find freedom and true life, the author goes on to enumerate four "warning lights" of self-righteousness, and challenges us to ask ourselves some questions.[10]

A Contemptuous View of Others. Do I compare myself with others and look down on those who do not live as I do? Of course, all the time! This tendency to compare my righteousness with others is endemic to humanity. Any level of contempt for others is a telltale sign of hidden self-righteousness."

A Shallow Sense of Forgiveness. How deep and well-developed is my personal sense of God's forgiveness? This subjective sense is another telltale symptom of my level of self-righteousness. Our personal awareness of God's forgiveness will profoundly impact our level of self-righteousness. Our response to sinners, particularly those who wrong us, is an excellent gauge to measure potentially self-righteous hearts.

A Wrong Sense of Grace and Fairness. How do I respond to working hard and being ignored when the less-deserving are rewarded and promoted? Fairness is a sense learned early in life; in fact, fairness is one of the most well-developed senses of a child. …But grace and fairness do not mix well. Grace by definition is unfair. It extends favor to the undeserving.

An Unhealthy View of Failure. How do I respond to failure or being exposed as a sinner? … What do we do when we are exposed, when we fail or are found out? Do we fall prostrate before God or do we attack the prophet?"

If you don't find at least a couple of these warning lights uncomfortably exposing the deeper recesses of your heart, I strongly encourage you to ask God to open your eyes to greater spiritual self-awareness. This is not a request God is likely ever to refuse!

Repenting, Again

God is always faithful to his children. Therefore whenever necessary, he will not hesitate to break our spiritual pride. Only when by grace we have cast off our Pharisaical self-righteousness are we ready to be freshly clothed in Christ's righteousness. Only when God brings us to deep brokenness—so we realize just how corrupt our hearts really are—are we ready and willing to be rebuilt by him. Only then can we turn away from the self-worship of self-reliant performance and back to the unmerited favor of God's infinite grace.

Every good thing we have and are is the result of God's grace. See how one anonymous believer prayed to God, the searcher of hearts.

It is a good day to me when thou givest me a glimpse
of myself;
Sin is my greatest evil, but thou art my greatest good;
I have cause to loath myself, and not to seek self-
honor, for no one desires to commend his own
dunghill.
My country, family, church fare worse because of my
sins, for sinners bring judgment in thinking sins are
small, or that God is not angry with them.[11]

That eye-opening "good day" is the day of grace. It
is the day when we realize just how much we have been
honoring ourselves for our spiritual maturity. It is the day
when we decide to stop celebrating our own dunghill. It is
the day when we experience a degree of spiritual brokenness and repent before God.

How we view ourselves before God massively
influences how we come before him in prayer. We either
approach him as a self-congratulating Pharisee or as a
spiritually bankrupt sinner. We approach either by faith
in him or faith in ourselves. God will not hear prayers that
come from a heart of self-worth, but he is faithful to help
us change, that we might once again live by the opening
words of the greatest sermon ever preached.

"Blessed are the poor in spirit, for theirs is the
kingdom of heaven" (Matthew 5:3).

God rejects the prayers of the self-satisfied
and the self-righteous,
but accepts the prayers of the humble and broken.

❖ ❖ ❖

HEAVENLY FATHER, forgive me for my pride and the
many religious sins that flow from its ongoing pursuit of
self-glory. You alone are worthy of honor and praise. O,
make me crave the reward of your pleasure alone, which
weans me from the seemingly unconscious pursuit of the
praise of men.

SERVANT JESUS, thank you for the perfection of your
humble example in which you always sought the glory
of the Father. Your words expose the self-worshiping
tendencies of my heart, making me realize once again
how bankrupt I am without the abundance of your grace.
Thank you for making yourself poor for my sake, in order
that I may become a co-heir of your spiritual riches.

HOLY SPIRIT, change my heart. Purge me of any
desire for the praise of men, any trace of self-honoring
lusts. Produce within me a heart of humility and grace.
Cause me to never forget my lowliness as a sinner, devoid
of any righteousness of my own before the holy God, nor
my exalted position as a saint who is clothed in the sinless
righteousness of Christ, my Savior.

Amen.

Six
INCONSIDERATE HUSBANDS

A Man's Failure to Understand and Honor His Wife

Since my conversion from dead religion to the risen Christ in 1984, there is nothing I have wanted more than God's profound favor upon my life. Therefore as a husband, I find the focal verse of this chapter deeply sobering: "Likewise, husbands, live with your wives in an understanding way, showing honor to the woman as the weaker vessel, since they are heirs with you of the grace of life, so that your prayers may not be hindered" (1 Peter 3:7).

This verse reminds us of the lesson we learned in chapter four: A person's relationship with God is affected by his or her relationships with others. It also provides a massive incentive for every Christian husband to learn to love and honor his wife.

The "likewise" at the start of this verse links this exhortation to Peter's previous exhortations addressed to citizens (2:13-17), servants (2:18), and wives (3:1-6). In each case, Peter calls his readers to a life of submission motivated by the desire to imitate the example of Jesus, so that the gospel might be made visible (2:19-25). The teaching directed at husbands is a sober call to submit to God by being a considerate leader.

We must be clear what we mean by a husband who is considerate and understanding and honors his wife. It does not mean he is called to passively go with the flow and allow his wife to lead the marriage and household. Nor does it mean he is called to actively assure that she always gets what pleases her. Either approach would represent a relinquishment of the husband's God-given authority and responsibility for which he will one day give an account to God. A faithful husband must lead his wife, loving her as Christ loves the church and actively looking out for her welfare—and sometimes this will mean making decisions that do not please her or even aggravate in her the willfulness each of us carries in our hearts.

The challenge facing every Christian husband who desires to be godly is to love his wife by both leading her confidently and loving her gently. Because every husband-in-the-making still wrestles daily with his own serve-me-first depravity, this challenge cannot be met without the empowering grace of God. But as a husband submits to the Lord and pursues obedience to this call by walking in the Spirit, his efforts will please the Lord. As he grows in this important role, his obedience will remove one principal reason for his prayers being hindered.

Let's look briefly at the two main components of Peter's exhortation to husbands: that they understand their wives and honor them.

Understand

For a husband to live with his wife "in an understanding way" means to dwell with her according to knowledge and consideration. The word translated "understanding" may refer to Christian insight as well as tact. This is a clarion call for a man to mix humility, kindness, wisdom, and clear biblical leadership into a single attitude of heart and mind. To live in ignorance of a wife's spiritual, mental, emotional, and physical condition, or to be uncaring about what it means to lead and love her as Christ does the church, this is disobedience to God.

The basis for Peter's command is that the wife is a "weaker vessel" in comparison to her husband. In today's social climate, this phrase can be controversial or even offensive among those who misinterpret its meaning. But Peter had no negative implications in mind.

> The word "vessel" is the translation of a word referring to a vessel used in the services of the temple (Mark 11:16), also to household utensils. The English word comes from a Latin word *vassellum*, the diminutive form of *vas*, a vase, the Latin words referring to a receptacle which covers and contains. Thus, the word comes to refer to an instrument whereby something is accomplished. The husband is to dwell with his wife, remembering that she is an instrument of God as well as the husband, a child of God to be used by him to his glory. The husband must always keep in mind that she is the weaker instrument of the two, not morally or intellectually, but physically. Therefore, this attitude

toward the wife on the part of the husband includes loving consideration of the wife in view of the fact that she is not physically as strong as he is.[12]

A husband and wife are both "vessels," tools or implements designed to accomplish God's will. Especially in an era where muscle power was far more important to the accomplishment of daily activities than it is today, the reference to the wife being weaker is simply an acknowledgment and a reminder to husbands of what is true in the vast majority of cases.

This reminder has at least two applications. On the one hand, the husband is to look out for his wife's physical well-being, making sure she is not overburdened with physical labor. But the husband must also refrain from using his physical strength as a means of imposing his will on his wife through manhandling or physical coercion. This would be a gross misapplication of his leadership role. Any husband who does this disobeys God, misrepresents Jesus Christ, and grieves the Holy Spirit, all of which leads to unanswered prayer.

Honor

A husband must also hold his wife in high esteem. In the culture of Peter's day, women were considered inferior to men. Peter's command was therefore a significant elevation of women and a bold challenge to the ungodly status quo. Through this passage, a husband of that era came to understand just how radical was this faith he had come to embrace. Instead of treating his wife as a second-class citizen, here he is commanded to grant her "honor." This means to hold her in high regard due to recognition of her intrinsic worth. Of course, in a day when many husbands take better care of their cars than they do their wives, this command still has profound relevance.

Peter summarizes his command by pressing husbands to see their wives as fundamentally equal before God. A believing wife is indeed a fellow heir of the grace of life and should be treated as equal to her husband in value and status before God. Christ died for all believers equally (Galatians 3:28). This does not eliminate the husband's headship or the distinct and honorable God-given role of the wife as submissive helper. Instead, it highlights how the gospel removes all superficial distinctions with regard to inheriting salvation. Each person must come to God by faith in Christ, regardless of gender. As a result, a husband must never treat his wife as if she is spiritually inferior, for she is not. Like him, she is an heir of God and fellow heir with Christ (Romans 8:17), a daughter of the King of kings!

A husband who has dishonored his wife or been inconsiderate toward her has disobeyed God's clear command: "Husbands, love your wives, and do not be harsh with them" (Colossians 3:19). "Harsh" is rendered "embittered" in some translations, which reveals the unpleasant heart attitude that often feeds unkind words and actions. Husbands given to harshness or bitterness must repent of this specific form of disobedience to God, confess their sin to God and to their wives, and ask the forgiveness of both.

As a husband learns to walk in obedience to God, by the Spirit's empowerment, the Father's ears will once again be opened to his prayers. May every husband commit to the ongoing process of becoming a gentle, considerate leader so that his prayers are not hindered.

*God rejects the prayers of the husband
who dishonors his wife,
but receives the prayers of the husband
who lives with her in an understanding way.*

✣ ✣ ✣

HEAVENLY FATHER, forgive me for not cherishing and honoring my wife as a priceless treasure, a gift to me, from you. Forgive me for my selfish, lazy, and impatient spirit, which so often will not take the time and effort needed to live with her in an understanding way. Help me always to view her as a co-heir of the grace of life and to treat her as your daughter. Help me to be tender and confident, but not harsh.

LORD JESUS, you love your bride—the church—in such a sacrificial way, always looking out for her best interest. When your loyal love for her moves you toward correction, you do so with tenderness and patience. You are at all times the perfect blend of grace and truth. You do not avoid truthful confrontation, for that would not be love, nor do you heap correction on her without affirming your affection and steadfast commitment to her. Help me to faithfully follow your example.

Spirit of Jesus, you empowered the Savior during his earthly life, enabling him to—at all times—love as no one on earth had ever loved before. The Scripture that you inspired says that you will cause me to bear your fruit—love, joy, peace, patience, kindness, goodness, faithfulness, gentleness, and self-control—as I walk in your power and ways. Please produce these fruits in my life, most obviously in my relationship with my wife.

Amen.

Seven
STUBBORN PRIDE

The Insistence on Going it Alone

God listens to those who listen to him. The proof of this is all over Scripture. Isaiah 66:2 offers a prime example when God says, "this is the one to whom I will look: he who is humble and contrite in spirit and trembles at my word" (Isaiah 66:2). Even more direct is a warning given by Zechariah.

Zechariah was a minor prophet who had a major impact, foretelling both the first and second comings of the Messiah. He was also employed by God to call the Israelites to repentance. Zechariah lived in the time following Israel's exile, after the people had returned from Babylon. His name means "The Lord remembers," and through his voice the Lord assured his own that, although he had chastened them for 70 years in Babylon, ha had not forgotten them or the covenant he made with their forefathers.

Undoubtedly, Zechariah had heard of the captivity from his father, Iddo, who had returned to Jerusalem under the leadership of Zerubbabel and the high priest Joshua.

Zechariah learned how the Persian king Cyrus had freed the captive Israelites and let them return to the Promised Land. By Zechariah's time about 50,000 Israelites had returned to Jerusalem, and the rebuilding of the Temple, which had been destroyed by Nebuchadnezzar, had begun. However, the rebuilding effort quickly met with opposition from without and discouragement from within. As a result, all work on the Temple simply ceased for more than a decade.

God then appointed two prophets, Zechariah and Haggai, to call his people back to himself. Both men confronted dead religion. Haggai's message focused on the rebuilding of the physical Temple while Zechariah admonished the people, saying, "Return to me, says the LORD of hosts, and I will return to you" (Zechariah 1:3). Two evidences of Israel's backsliding were obvious.

First, they would not listen to the prophets whom God had sent. Zechariah had hardly picked up his quill when he warned: "Do not be like your fathers, to whom the former prophets cried out, 'Thus says the LORD of hosts, return from your evil ways and from your evil deeds.' But they did not hear or pay attention to me, declares the LORD" (Zechariah 1:4). Their rebellion displayed itself by an inattentiveness to God's message. They had closed their ears to his prophets and effectively silenced God with their prideful independence.

Second, their religion had degenerated into mere outward performance. Following eight visions concerning the condition of Israel and the judgment to come, the prophet exposed their hypocrisy by asking pointed questions.

Then the word of the Lord of hosts came to me: "Say to all the people of the land and the priests, when you fasted and mourned in the fifth month and in the seventh, for these seventy years, was it for me that you fasted? And when you eat and when you drink, do you not eat for yourselves and drink for yourselves?" (Zechariah 7:4-6).

Rather than longing for God their hearts had become hardened against him. As a result, their fasting and feasting were done for their own pleasure, not God's glory. Divine correction was required to lead the people to repentance. Their greatest need was not more religion, but brokenness, repentance, and faith.

What was the root cause of their mechanical rituals and their refusal to listen to God? It was the stubbornness of pride. The prophet repeats his initial description of his people.

But they refused to pay attention and turned a stubborn shoulder and stopped their ears from hearing. They made their hearts like flint so that they could not hear the law and the words which the Lord of hosts had sent by his Spirit through the former prophets (7:11-12; NASB).

There is a tragic progression to be found in this glimpse of Israelite rebellion. At first they were simply willful in their opposition to God. They "refused to pay attention … turned a stubborn shoulder … stopped their ears." All this was under their control. But soon things moved beyond their control. Their hearts became rock-hard, "like flint so that they *could not* hear." They started out *refusing* to yield to God and ended up *unable* to yield to God. Their *could not* was caused by their *will not*.

It gets worse from there. As a result, "great anger came from the Lord of hosts" (v 12), and then, in the most sobering words in the prophet's entire book, God said, "As I called, and they would not hear, so they called, and I would not hear" (v 13).

The window of opportunity to repent had been shut.

Five Evidences of Stubbornness

Our self-sufficient pride, our persistent refusal to listen and yield to God, can close his ears to our prayers. With the pride of independence lurking deeply in each of our hearts, we must acknowledge the possibility that what was true of the Israelites can become true of us today, despite the fact that we call ourselves God's people.

God is not an impulsive tyrant. This tragic progression does not happen overnight. Scripture provides at least five evidences of stubborn pride by which we can be forewarned and equipped to turn from our stubborn rebellion.

- Slowness to admit wrong
- A mule-like spirit
- Increasing disobedience to God
- Resistance to correction
- Demanding our own way

The first two of these are illustrated by David in Psalm 32, which begins with a declaration of the blessedness of being forgiven. "Blessed is the one whose transgression is forgiven, whose sin is covered. Blessed is the man against whom the LORD counts no iniquity, and in whose spirit there is no deceit" (Psalm 32:1-2).

When David penned these words he was a happy man—a man who knew what it was like to be cleansed by God. But he had not always been happy. At one time, stubbornness had robbed him of his joy. What did this stubbornness look like? That was a very different picture.

Slowness to Admit Wrong

One evidence of David's stubborn heart was his slowness to admit sin. This aspect of David's pride led to much grief.

- **Verse 3:** "For when I kept silent, my bones wasted away through my groaning all day long." His sin affected him physically—the weight of God's discipline and his guilty conscience drained his body of strength.
- **Verse 4:** "For day and night your hand was heavy upon me; my strength was dried up as by the heat of summer." I relate to this picture well, since I know what it is to wilt in the summer heat. A hot, humid day zaps me of energy, and so it is with the stubborn refusal to confess sin.
- **Verse 5:** But when David finally chose to get honest with God, he "acknowledged [his] sin ... [and] did not cover [his] iniquity."

- **Verse 6:** In light of the lessons he learned from God's discipline, David's words now counsel us, "Therefore let everyone who is godly offer prayer to you at a time when you may be found." The godly person is the one who acknowledges his sin because he fears the Lord. "The fear of the LORD is hatred of evil" (Proverbs 8:13), especially our own.
- **Verse 7:** What a comfort, then, to know that when we take our sin to God with a repentant heart he becomes our safe "hiding place" as we are covered by his mercy and love!

A Mule-like Spirit

A second evidence of stubbornness is an unteachable spirit, one that is unwilling to obey. Again, having seen this in his own life, David counsels us in Psalm 32.

- **Verses 8-10:** "I will instruct you and teach you in the way you should go; I will counsel you with my eye upon you. Be not like a horse or a mule, without understanding, which must be curbed with bit and bridle, or it will not stay near you. Many are the sorrows of the wicked, but steadfast love surrounds the one who trusts in the LORD."

Like Judah in the days of Zechariah, who had "turned a stubborn shoulder" and "refused to pay attention" (Zechariah 7:11), David had for a time refused to submit to God's ways. This did not lead to a blessed life, so David warns us not to behave as he did by taking a mule-like attitude toward God. David knows, and he wants us to know, that this will shut our ears to the conviction of the Holy Spirit.

Increasing Disobedience to God

Psalm 78 looks back over Israel's history to convince the then-current generation not to do as their forefathers did. In verses 5-8 we can see how our stubbornness makes it easier for us to disobey God, leaving us more vulnerable to greater sin.

He established a testimony in Jacob and appointed a law in Israel, which he commanded our fathers to teach to their children, 6 that the next generation might know them, the children yet unborn, and arise and tell them to their children, 7 so that they should set their hope in God and not forget the works of God, but keep his commandments; 8 and that they should not be like their fathers, a stubborn and rebellious generation, a generation whose heart was not steadfast, whose spirit was not faithful to God (Psalm 78:5-8).

We see in verse 8 that Israel's stubbornness produced unfaithfulness. And you can't expect a people who are being blatantly unfaithful to God to pass on faithfulness to their children. Our stubbornness affects others around us, and this can have a multigenerational impact.

Resistance to Correction

A fourth evidence of spiritual stubbornness is illustrated in

2 Chronicles 24. Jehoiada, high priest during the reign of Joash, was a champion of righteousness. After his death, the leaders of Judah convinced Joash to return to his idolatrous ways and "they abandoned the house of the LORD, the God of their fathers, and served the Asherim and the idols" (v 18).

Consequently, God sent prophets to testify against their sin and call them to repentance. But they would not listen. A prophet named Zechariah (not the same Zechariah we read about earlier) then said to the people, "Thus says God, 'Why do you break the commandments of the LORD, so that you cannot prosper? Because you have forsaken the LORD, he has forsaken you'" (v 20). But they did not listen. Instead, they stoned him in the courts of the temple (v 21; c.f. Matthew 23:35). Why was he stoned? Why did Israel and Judah kill so many of the prophets? They were "stiff-necked people, uncircumcised in heart … always [resisting] the Holy Spirit" (Acts 7:51). It was the stubbornness of pride that fueled their resistance.

Beware. Stubbornness steels your heart against correction, making you unwilling to listen to the people whom God places in your life who faithfully speak "the truth in love" (Ephesians 4:15).

Demanding Our Own Way

A fifth sad evidence of stubbornness is that, when not recognized and repented of, it demands its own way, even if that way is not God's will. An illustration of this is found in 1 Samuel 8. Though Samuel's sons should have taken over as leaders when their father retired, they had become so disgraceful that the nation wanted nothing to do with them. As a result, the people demanded of Samuel, "Behold, you are old and your sons do not walk in your ways. Now appoint for us a king to judge us like all the nations" (1 Samuel 8:5). Displeased, Samuel prayed. "And the LORD said to Samuel, 'Obey the voice of the people in all that they say to you, for they have not rejected you, but they have rejected me from being king over them'" (1 Samuel 8:7). God gave them what they wanted.

Even though Samuel warned that a king would take their sons for war, their daughters for cooks and bakers, their fields, and a tenth of their grain and flocks as taxes, still they would not listen. As a result, he also warned, "And in that day you will cry out because of your king, whom you have chosen for yourselves, but the LORD will not answer you in that day" (1 Samuel 8:18). The Lord chose not to listen to the prayers of his own people because they had refused to listen to him. Their stubborn pride had turned the heavens to brass because they would not listen to God's warnings. Getting their own way was more important to them than doing God's will, and the price they paid was high.

Let this be a warning to all of us. When we willfully choose to be stubborn against God's correction, we become slaves to our own pride and our fellowship with God is interrupted.

The Way Back

The only solution is humility. Peter counsels us, "Clothe yourselves, all of you, with humility toward one another, for 'God opposes the proud but gives grace to the humble.' Humble yourselves, therefore, under the mighty hand of God so that at the proper time he may exalt you" (1 Peter 5:5-6).

The psalmist concurs: "The sacrifices of God are a broken spirit; a broken and contrite heart, O God, you will not despise" (Psalm 51:17). God loves the humility of a contrite heart. Even when our hearts have grown so hard that we cannot hear the call of God in our spirits, there is still hope, there is still something we can do. We can repent of our stubbornness and pride and bow before him in tender humility. When we do, he opens his ears wide to listen, and stands ready to act on our behalf.

> *God rejects the prayers of those*
> *who reject correction and go their own way,*
> *but receives the prayers of the humble*
> *who admit their need for God and his guidance.*

❖ ❖ ❖

PATIENT FATHER, thank you for being such a longsuffering God. You were so patient with your people in the past, and your patience continues with me today. How many times have I rebelled against your ways? How many times have I stubbornly resisted correction and demanded my own way, thinking I was the wiser? Thank you for your patient persistence with me and your kindness that continues to lead me to repentance.

LORD JESUS, I praise you for always being perfectly submissive to the Father. Instead of stubbornly demanding your glory, which you rightly deserve, you willingly concealed it within human flesh so that you could be my Savior. Thank you for taking your sinless, submissive life to the cross as full atonement for my sins and rising again victorious.

HOLY SPIRIT, thank you for replacing my hardened heart of stone, which left me deaf to your call, with a softened heart of flesh, which repents, believes, and desires to obey. Make me to be ever-conscious of my pride and ever-sensitive to the Word so that I do not grieve you, or quench your work in my heart.

Amen.

Eight
TESTING OUR FAITH

God's Loving Incentives to Spiritual Growth

In the preceding chapters we have explored five kinds of sinful acts and attitudes that Scripture tells us can hinder our prayers. There may be other sin-related reasons for unanswered prayer, but if so they are arguably less clear in Scripture. Before we finish, however, it is vital to consider one last potential cause of the heavens becoming as brass, this cause being abundantly clear throughout Scripture.

As God performs his sanctifying work in us—conforming us to the image of his Son, "the founder and perfecter of our faith" (Hebrews 12:2)—there will be times when answers to prayer seem out of all possible reach. When we try to discern the cause for this, we may find that self-examination doesn't help. Maybe we have been diligent in trying to kick our pet sins out of the house, we're unaware of any ongoing conflicts or offenses with other believers, and we've been fighting diligently against self-righteousness and an independent spirit. Nevertheless, it seems that God has closed his ears to our cries.

That's when we may begin to ask a question that God's people have been raising for millennia.

How Long, O Lord?

This question is asked in ten different portions of the book of Psalms. Isaiah sought an answer to it, as did Jeremiah, Habakkuk, and Zechariah. Surely the Hebrews asked it as they languished in slavery in Egypt for 400 years. Surely the Israelites asked it as they wandered in the desert watching an entire generation die off. Undoubtedly the captives asked it in Babylon during their 70-year exile. Perplexed and weary believers in Christ certainly ask it every day in various forms, and have been doing so since the resurrection. Indeed, all creation asks continually "How long, O Lord?" as it groans, yearning for the return of the Lord and the completion of all things (Romans 8:22).

One answer spans across every expression of that question, in whatever age it may be asked: the delay is there because God is at work, and the delay itself is serving his purposes.

Let's think about this matter of delay. Imagine if all our prayers were answered swiftly and we never had to wait. It would be as if we each had a genie in a bottle who gives endless wishes. Our prayers would be more like commands than requests, and God would be rightly called our servant in heaven.

We would never endure any lingering, ongoing, bothersome challenges and difficulties. Everyone would be healthy, wealthy, and biblically wise. We would feel great all the time, our jobs would be wonderful, the weather report would always be accurate, and even civil governments would work right. We would be living as if there had never been any original sin, as if we were still in the garden before Adam and Eve fell.

And that means we would never have any reason to change.

Unfortunately, in nearly every case, discontentment is necessary for our sanctification. God often leaves our prayers unanswered so that we might become increasingly conformed to the image of his Son. Unanswered prayer is a gift from God for our growth—in holiness and in every other good and godly way—and sometimes it has nothing to do with whether we are hanging on to any of the sins described in chapters three through seven.

Let's take a moment to consider just three places in Scripture where God's purposeful delay for our good does not appear to be tied to any specific sin or form of sin.

Petitions

Psalm 13 David's need is urgent in this psalm. He is depressed and filled with sorrow all day long as his enemy is exalted over him. He is shaken and at his wits' end. By wondering how long God will ignore him, David admits to deep-seated feelings of being unable to endure his trial any longer.

> How long, O LORD? Will you forget me forever? How long will you hide your face from me? How long must I take counsel in my soul and have sorrow in my heart all the day? How long shall my enemy be exalted

over me? Consider and answer me, O LORD my God;
light up my eyes, lest I sleep the sleep of death, lest my
enemy say, "I have prevailed over him," lest my foes
rejoice because I am shaken (Psalm 13:1-4).

Psalm 89 Ethan the Ezrahite begins this psalm by
singing of "the steadfast love of the LORD" (v 1) as he
recounts the faithfulness of God through Israel's history
up to the reign of David. At the time of the psalm's writing,
however, we see that David's kingly rule is significantly
threatened and God's ear appears to have been closed.
Ethan asks, "How long, O LORD? Will you hide yourself
forever?" (v 46). Clearly, his faith is struggling. Why is
God not listening? Why has he not yet taken action? Why
the delay? Has God forgotten his covenant? The wait
has been so long that he even fears he will die before God
answers, "Remember how short my time is!" (v 47).

Luke 18:1-8 Here Jesus told a parable about
an oppressed but persistent widow who repeatedly
beseeched an unrighteous judge for protection from
inhumane treatment. Unmoved by her numerous pleas
for help, the judge ignored her.

Results

Psalm 13 Although the situation itself has not changed,
David chooses to trust God that help is on the way. As a
result, he perseveres in prayer. He even sings. "But I have
trusted in your steadfast love; my heart shall rejoice in your
salvation. I will sing to the LORD, because he has dealt boun-
tifully with me" (Psalm 13:5-6). The trial of enduring God's

silence without becoming bitter accomplished its work. It changed the affections of David's heart and deepened his faith. This is infinitely more valuable to his spiritual well-being than always receiving immediate answers.

Psalm 89 Whatever else God was accomplishing in Ethan the Ezrahite's tortured soul, we know that this psalmist walked away from his trial with a deeper, more mature faith. Strengthened by the trial of God's silence he resolved, "I will make known your faithfulness to all generations" (v 1).

Luke 18:1-8 After a time, the judge in the parable gave in to the widow simply to gain relief from her incessant requests. As Jesus draws our attention to the value of perseverance, faith, and steadfastness, he goes on to promise that God will surely honor persevering prayer that is in keeping with his will. Yet he seems to suggest that some of these prayers will nevertheless remain unanswered until Christ's return. Remember that "with the Lord one day is as a thousand years, and a thousand years as one day" (2 Peter 3:8).

Yes, God does hear the cries of his children and he desires to help them. Why the wait, then?

Here we have three scriptural instances in which we are encouraged to continue seeking God when an answer is withheld, even in the absence of any evidence of overt sin. In one of these examples the petitioner is granted her request after some prolonged period of time. In two examples the petitioners do not receive their request, but they clearly grow in faith.

In any given instance of challenge or difficulty, God may or may not be interested in changing the circumstances. But he is always interested in changing us. Yet the patience, faith in God, and steadfastness necessary for change do not come naturally. We are all prone to give up easily or look for shortcuts. But God desires for his children to possess steadfast faith that does not give up easily when prayer is left unanswered.

The Mystery of Testing

You hear this phrase all the time in the context of trials: God is "testing our faith." Christians rightly talk about tests of faith because James uses the phrase in his epistle (James 1:3). But do we know what we mean by it? And do we mean the same thing James did?

One implication that James did not have in mind, and that we shouldn't either, is that God isn't quite clear on the status of our faith, so he has to conduct some kind of experiment. Obviously that's not what's going on. God knows the condition of our faith far better than we do.

The testing is entirely for our sake. It's not that God doesn't know—it's that we forget. We forget that life is fundamentally a spiritual activity that *includes* a physical dimension. It is not fundamentally a physical activity with a spiritual component tacked on to add a little mystery. Our faith is our life, and the status of our faith is the most important thing about us. The tests of faith that God sends our way are reminders to keep us focused on what is true and real and primary.

We need these regular reminders because the world relentlessly tugs and pulls us back toward believing in an existence that is fundamentally built on the mechanical, the material, and the physical, with the spiritual set aside as secondary. But the testing of our faith recalibrates our hearts, adjusting them so that they better perceive reality as it truly is—a place where God rules according to his purposes. This grows our faith so we become more like David in Psalm 13 and Ethan the Ezrahite in Psalm 89, and it teaches us perseverance so we become more like the widow in the parable of Luke 18.

Of Moths and Men

For our faith to grow to maturity, therefore, there must be this kind of testing, and this can happen quite effectively when God remains silent in times of trial. In these seasons God may make us wait, not due to some persistent sin in our lives, but simply because there is additional sanctifying and stabilizing work to be accomplished within us before we are ready to receive his answer. In *Trusting God, Even When Life Hurts,* Jerry Bridges provides a compelling illustration of the necessary relationship between the testing of our faith, which includes the trial of God's silence, and the development of perseverance. He writes:

> One of the many fascinating events in nature is the emergence of the Cecropia moth from its cocoon—an event that occurs only with much struggle on the part of the moth to free itself. The story is frequently told of someone who watched a moth go through this struggle. In an effort to help—and not realizing the necessity of the struggle—the viewer snipped the shell of the cocoon. Soon the moth came out with its wings

all crimped and shriveled. But as the person watched, the wings remained weak. The moth, which in a few moments would have stretched those wings to fly, was now doomed to crawling out its brief life in frustration of ever being the beautiful creature God created it to be.

What the person in the story did not realize was that the struggle to emerge from the cocoon was an essential part of developing the muscle system of the moth's body and pushing the body fluids out into the wings to expand them. By unwisely seeking to cut short the moth's struggle, the watcher had actually crippled the moth and doomed its existence.

Bridges then rightly makes this application to believers:

We can be sure that the development of a beautiful Christlike character will not occur in our lives without adversity. … However, we shrink from adversity and, to use the terms from the moth illustration, we want God to snip the cocoon of adversity we often find ourselves in and release us.[13]

Thankfully, God is wiser than that. He will not snip the cocoon. Instead, he will let us wrestle through our challenges in order to bring us to stronger faith and a deeper level of trust.

So we see that God tests our faith in order to affirm its reality in our own eyes. Each trial of unanswered prayer is designed to turn our eyes to God and away from ourselves. If such a trial exposes our impatience with God's timing, frustration with his methods or plan, or any other subtle trace of unbelief hidden in our hearts, it has done a greater service to our progress in sanctification than we can imagine. As our attention is captured by the struggle before us, we are redirected to deeper spiritual realities, and as we see these more clearly, we grow in spiritual maturity. Like the moth struggling to emerge from its cocoon, the wrestling of our faith is absolutely necessary for our proper development as Christians. Without it, our faith remains forever weak, immature, and ineffectual.

The Godly Response to Delay

What then is the right, godly, and biblical response when we face trials of unanswered prayer? In a word, perseverance. To quote the passage from James referred to above: "Count it all joy, my brothers, when you meet trials of various kinds, for you know that the testing of your faith produces steadfastness. And let steadfastness have its full effect, that you may be perfect and complete, lacking in nothing" (James 1:2-4).

It can be almost astonishing to realize what James is saying here: The primary purpose of trials—and this certainly includes delays in answer to prayer—is not that circumstances might change or other people might change. The primary purpose of *our* trials is that *we* might change.

James is referring to the sort of change that follows from *steadfastness*. This word depicts someone who has been carrying a heavy load for a long time, and rather than

seeking an escape, just keeps on going. This is perseverance of a particular kind—the discipline of choosing to
remain under a burden, resisting the temptation to try to
slip out from under it. Like the moth emerging from the
cocoon, this kind of perseverance strengthens our faith,
thus making it more muscular, more authentic.

Apparently, change doesn't come to us easily or
quickly. Apparently, we have to labor under a burden for
a considerable period of time before something significant
happens. Apparently, this is just the way life is among
sinners in a fallen world.

To help us in what is admittedly a challenging task,
James specifies two continuous activities that cooperate
with this process of spiritual maturation in the face of trials.

- persevere in joy
- persevere in prayer

Persevere with an Attitude of Joy

The joy that James speaks of is rooted in the knowledge
that God's good and perfect will is sure to be carried out.
You and I are inclined by our sin nature to see trials as a
troublesome departure from the plan. In truth, the trial
is the plan—God's plan, not ours. The particular trial
in which we find ourselves at any given time is in fact
necessary to the particular outcome God is directing us
toward in that season.

Such joy does not necessarily manifest itself in some
predictable way. The evidence of it can vary from person
to person and is not always outwardly obvious. The

joy that comes from an assurance that God is about the business of doing us good in all things is not a matter of putting on a happy face or pretending there is no pain in suffering. True joy is not a spiritual façade, but a deep inner peace and contentment that flows from confident faith.

Persevere by Continuing to Ask in Faith

When we face a trial of unanswered prayer, a trial that drags on far longer than we would prefer, there are only two ways we can respond. We either show our dependence on God through continuing to pray, or we demonstrate our hearts of independence from God as we sin against him by ceasing to pray (1 Samuel 12:23).

In the face of an extended trial, when the heavens are as brass, we may have no idea what God is trying to accomplish. In the absence of a clear intention on God's part, it may well be that all we can cling to is God's sovereignty and faithfulness. We may find ourselves leaning on passages like Psalm 115:3 ("Our God is in the heavens; he does all that he pleases"), Psalm 11:7 ("The LORD is righteous"), and Psalm 27:13 ("I believe that [one day] I shall look upon the goodness of the LORD in the land of the living!").

In the anguish of our souls, it is a wonder at those times that we even possess enough faith to pray. Indeed, we may find ourselves repeating the words voiced by the father of the boy possessed with an unclean spirit, "I believe; help my unbelief!" (Mark 9:24). But in those moments, that can be exactly what persevering faith looks like, as tissue-thin and insubstantial as it may seem at the time. As we continue to come to God in prayer, proclaiming that even in this mysterious circumstance he is sovereign, faithful, and good, this actually is prayer "in faith with no doubting" (James 1:6).

To persevere in faith even as we wait—this is God's desire for us. Indeed, this is the kind of mature faith that Hiebert defines as "the wholehearted attitude of a full and unquestioning committal to and dependence upon God."[14] This is like the faith of the woman with the twelve-year hemorrhage who pressed through the crowds just to touch the hem of Jesus' garment. She simply rested, in wholehearted dependence, upon the goodness of God (Mark 5:25-34).

God wants us to make up our minds. He wants us to trust in him even when things don't go the way we hope, or expect, or think they should. God is our loving heavenly Father who delights to come to our aid *when and how it is actually best for us*. You can be certain that he will do what it takes to produce in us the perseverance that leads to God's unique reward. "Blessed" is the believer "who remains steadfast under trial, for when he has stood the test he will receive the crown of life, which God has promised to those who love him" (James 1:12). This perseverance is not what gains us eternal life—that comes to us as a gift flowing from Christ's finished work on the cross—but it does demonstrate that our faith is authentic, and authentic faith *will* receive its reward.

And what about those delays that last a lifetime? What about when the answer never comes at all? That is when we also grow in our understanding of how thoroughly fallen this world is, and that all our longings are ultimately longings for God and his perfections. When we face a lifelong struggle with unanswered prayer on the basis of a solid grounding in the gospel, we become more grateful for Jesus our Savior, who gave all that we might one day be rescued from this fallen world.

Indeed, as commendable and necessary as are perseverance and endurance, these are not God's final goal. His goal is to make us "perfect and complete, lacking in nothing" (James 1:4), mature, according "to the measure of the stature of the fullness of Christ" (Ephesians 4:13). This goal can only be reached as we, like Christ, learn to endure trials "for the joy that was set before" us (Hebrews 12:2).

There are no short-cuts to spiritual maturity. Fully developed faith can only be brought about by a long, difficult process involving trials which produce perseverance, and perseverance has an eternal reward.

Charles Spurgeon exhorted the members of his church with these words.

> Never give up praying, not even though Satan should suggest to you that it is in vain for you to cry unto God. Pray in his teeth; "pray without ceasing." If for awhile the heavens are as brass and your prayer only echoes in thunder above your head, pray on; if month after month your prayer appears to have miscarried, and no reply has been vouchsafed to you, yet still continue to draw nigh unto the Lord. Do not abandon the mercy-seat for any reason whatever. If it be a good thing that you have been asking for, and you are sure it is according to the divine will, if the

vision tarry wait for it, pray, weep, entreat, wrestle,
agonise till you get that which you are praying for. If
your heart be cold in prayer, do not restrain prayer
until your heart warms, but pray your soul unto heat
by the help of the everblessed Spirit who helpeth our
infirmities. If the iron be hot then hammer it, and if it
be cold hammer it till you heat it. Never cease prayer
for any sort of reason or argument.[15]

❖ ❖ ❖

*HEAVENLY FATHER, thank you for not answering all of
my prayers as soon as they depart from my lips, for surely
you could. Even more, you could answer them before I
pray since you know my words before I speak them. But
you long for something more—the development of my
faith and the forming of me, a redeemed sinner, into the
image of your glorious Son.*

*LORD JESUS, thank you for being my wisdom and my
righteousness, the author and finisher of my faith. Thank
you for keeping the joy set before you so that you endured
the greatest trial of all—separation from the Father while
absorbing his wrath against my sin while you hung on that
cruel cross.*

*HOLY SPIRIT, thank you for being the Spirit of power.
Train me to trust myself less and rely upon your indwelling presence more. I am tired of responding to trials in a
less-than-joyful manner. It is time to change. Discipline my
mind with self-control so that I will set my mind on things
above, not things on this earth. Make me fit for heaven.*

Amen.

TEN THINGS THAT ARE TRUE WHEN I CONFESS MY SIN

What is sin? One definition is that sin is anything within me, or an action produced by me, which fails to bring glory to God (Romans 3:23). Whenever the Holy Spirit opens the eyes of your heart to see your sin, it is healthy to turn to the Scriptures to fill your mind with truth. One of the most helpful portions to deliberately meditate on is 1 John 1:8-2:2.

If we say we have no sin, we deceive ourselves, and the truth is not in us. 9 If we confess our sins, he is faithful and just to forgive us our sins and to cleanse us from all unrighteousness. 10 If we say we have not sinned, we make him a liar, and his word is not in us. 1 My little children, I am writing these things to you so that you may not sin. But if anyone does sin, we have an advocate with the Father, Jesus Christ the righteous. 2 He is the propitiation for our sins, and not for ours only but also for the sins of the whole world.

Here we discover ten significant truths that you and I affirm every time we acceptably confess sin to God. Ponder these thoughts concerning God, sin, grace, forgiveness, and the sufficiency of Christ and his sacrificial work on your behalf.

When I confess my sin...

1. *I acknowledge my innate sinfulness, not merely my "sins."* This is a very important reminder. I am not a sinner because I sin. Rather, I sin because I am a sinner. My sinfulness is directly linked to my connection with Adam (Romans 5:12). If I ever get to the point of believing that I "have no sin," then I have deceived myself.

2. *I demonstrate that God's truth is at work "in me."* To deny my innate sinfulness, or guilt concerning my sins, is to deny God and his truth and to admit that neither is in me.

3. *I fully agree with God that my thought, word, deed, motive, attitude, or any combination of them falls short of his glory.* To "confess" means to say the same thing, that is, to agree with God that his judgment concerning my sin is accurate.

4. *God's faithfulness and righteousness go to work on my behalf.* When I agree with God concerning my sin, then he acts according to his promises that he made on my behalf. When he forgives, God manifests that he is faithful and just.

5. *God releases me from my debt.* To "forgive" me means he lets go of my sin as an offense to him. He

no longer holds it against me or seeks to punish me because he has already punished his Son, which displayed his amazing love (see Romans 5:8).

6. *God washes my sinful heart and conscience.* He "cleanses" me from all sin. That is, he washes me again—in a fresh way—in the blood of Jesus, which was shed once for all (see Hebrews 7:27).

7. *I testify of God's truthfulness.* When I stubbornly refuse to humble myself and agree with God, then I "make Him a liar."

8. *I confirm that God's Word is at work "within me."* Dealing honestly with my sin before God and others is one of the evidences of my "new creature status" as a regenerated believer (2 Corinthians 5:17; James 1:18).

9. *Jesus steps up to be my righteous "advocate with the Father."* Jesus acts as my defense lawyer, bringing forth his wounded hands and feet as proof that my sin has already been paid for.

10. *I rest in the astounding sufficiency of the blood of Jesus, my propitiatory sacrifice.* Each and every time I rightly agree with God concerning the accuracy of his assessment of my sin, my wearied soul finds rest in the wondrous truth that my Jesus has already satisfied the righteous demands of the Father and absorbed his wrath. I also testify that the sacrifice of Jesus on the cross is sufficient for the sins of every man, woman, and child who ever has been or will be.

Endnotes

1. Henry C.Thiessen, *Lectures in SystematicTheology* (Grand Rapids:William B. Eerdmans Publishing Co., 1949), 228.

2. This section is adapted from a larger treatment of the subject in *Teach them to Pray*, Paul Tautges, 978-1-84625-196-2, © 2010, Day One Publications, www.dayone.co.uk, www.dayonebookstore.com. Used by permission.

3. Matthew Henry, *Matthew Henry's Commentary on the Whole Bible*, Vol. vi (McLean, VA: MacDonald [n.d.]), 422.

4. R. C. Sproul, *The Invisible Hand* (Phillipsburg, NJ: P&R, 2003), 209.

5. D. Edmond Hiebert, *James* (Chicago: Moody Press, 1979), 226.

6. Paul E. Miller, *A Praying Life* (Colorado Springs, CO: Nav-Press, 2009), 135.

7. This does not mean, however, that we will never struggle with the inner heart's assurance of our salvation. The weakness of our humanity sometimes produces doubt (on numerous occasions, Jesus addressed his disciples "O, you of little faith"), and the devil works overtime accusing us "day and night before our God" (Revelation 12:10).

8. *ESV Study Bible* (Wheaton, IL: Crossway Bibles, 2008), 1016.

9. Tom Hovestol, *Extreme Righteousness* (Colorado Springs: Authentic Media, 2008), 47.

10. Hovestol, 49-54.

11. Arthur Bennett, *The Valley of Vision* (Edinburgh: Banner of Truth Trust, 1975), 122.

12. Kenneth S. Wuest, *Wuest's Word Studies: First Peter* (Grand Rapids, MI: Eerdmans, 1942), 83.

13. Jerry Bridges, *Trusting God* (Colorado Springs: NavPress, 1988), 173-174.

14. Hiebert, 72.

15. C. H. Spurgeon, in the sermon titled "Pray Without Ceasing," (Sermon No. 1039). Delivered on Lord's Day Morning, March 10th, 1872, at the Metropolitan Tabernacle. http://www.spurgeon.org/sermons/1039.htm, accessed June 23, 2012.

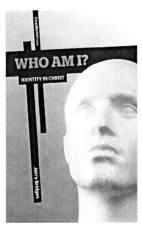

Who Am I?
Identity in Christ
by Jerry Bridges

Jerry Bridges unpacks Scripture to give the Christian eight clear, simple, interlocking answers to one of the most essential questions of life.

"Jerry Bridges' gift for simple but deep spiritual communication is fully displayed in this warm-hearted, biblical spelling out of the Christian's true identity in Christ."

J. I. Packer, Theological Editor, ESV Study Bible; author, Knowing God, A Quest for Godliness, Concise Theology

"I know of no one better prepared than Jerry Bridges to write *Who Am I?* He is a man who knows who he is in Christ and he helps us to see succinctly and clearly who we are to be. Thank you for another gift to the Church of your wisdom and insight in this book."

R.C. Sproul, founder, chairman, president, Ligonier Ministries; executive editor, Tabletalk magazine; general editor, The Reformation Study Bible

"*Who Am I?* answers one of the most pressing questions of our time in clear gospel categories straight from the Bible. This little book is a great resource to ground new believers and remind all of us of what God has made us through faith in Jesus. Thank the Lord for Jerry Bridges, who continues to provide the warm, clear, and biblically balanced teaching that has made him so beloved to this generation of Christians."

Richard D. Phillips, Senior Minister, Second Presbyterian Church, Greenville, SC

JOY!
A Bible Study on Philippians for Women

by Keri Folmar

One of the few truly inductive Bible studies intended for use by women.

"This study points the way into the biblical text, offering a clear and effective guide in studying Paul's letter to the Philippian church. Keri Folmar encourages her readers first and foremost to listen well to God's inspired Word."

> *Kathleen Nielson, author of the Living Word Bible Studies; Director of Women's Initiatives, The Gospel Coalition*

"Keri's Bible study will not only bring the truths of Philippians to bear upon your life, but will also train you up for better, more effective study of any book of the Bible with her consistent use of the three questions needed in all good Bible study: Observation, Interpretation, and Application."

> *Connie Dever, author of The Praise Factory children's ministry curriculum and wife of Pastor Mark Dever, President of 9 Marks Ministries*

""Keri lets the Scriptures do the talking! No cleverly invented stories, ancillary anecdotes, or emotional manipulation here. Keri takes us deeper into the text, deeper into the heart of Paul, deeper into the mind of Christ, and deeper into our own hearts as we pursue Christ for joy in all things. I highly commend this study for your pursuit of joy."

> *Kristie Anyabwile is a graduate of NC State University and wife of Thabiti, a Gospel Coalition Council Member*

The Organized Heart
A Woman's Guide to Conquering Chaos

by Staci Eastin

**Disorganized?
You don't need more rules, the
latest technique, or a new gadget.**

**This book will show you a different,
better way. A way grounded in the
grace of God.**

"Staci Eastin packs a gracious punch, full of insights about our disorganized hearts and lives, immediately followed by the balm of gospel-shaped hopes. This book is ideal for accountability partners and small groups."

> *Carolyn McCulley, blogger, filmmaker, author of* Radical Womanhood *and* Did I Kiss Marriage Goodbye?

"Unless we understand the spiritual dimension of productivity, our techniques will ultimately backfire. Find that dimension here. Encouraging and uplifting rather than guilt-driven, this book can help women who want to be more organized but know that adding a new method is not enough."

> *Matt Perman, Director of Strategy at Desiring God, blogger, author of the forthcoming book,* What's Best Next: How the Gospel Transforms the Way You Get Things Done

"Organizing a home can be an insurmountable challenge for a woman. The Organized Heart makes a unique connection between idols of the heart and the ability to run a well-managed home. This is not a how-to. Eastin looks at sin as the root problem of disorganization. She offers a fresh new approach and one I recommend, especially to those of us who have tried all the other self-help models and failed."

> *Aileen Challies, mom of three, and wife of blogger, author, and pastor Tim Challies*

Modest
Men and Women Clothed in the Gospel

by R W Glenn, Tim Challies

Modesty is about freedom, not rules.

What you say or do or wear is not really the point. The point is your heart.

True modesty flows from a solid grasp of the gospel.

"It is so refreshing to have a book on modesty that is a useful resource and not a legalistic, culture-bound list that leaves you a bit paranoid and guilty. No, this book is different. Its counsel on modesty is not rooted in rules, but in the grace of the gospel of Jesus Christ. That grace alone is able to get at the heart of the problem of modesty, which *is* the heart. In a culture where immodesty is the accepted norm, Glenn and Challies have given us help that every Christian desperately needs."
   Paul Tripp, pastor, conference speaker, and author

"How short is too short? How tight is too tight? Glenn and Challies don't say. But they do provide a thoughtful framework to help us come to a grace-based, gospel-grounded understanding of modesty that extends beyond mere clothing. They uphold a vision for modesty that's both beautiful and desirable — and not only for gals, but for guys too! This book is a great tool to help you wrestle with the practical question of what and what not to wear."
   Mary A. Kassian, Author, **Girls Gone Wise**

"The authors of Modest break new ground in their treatment of this difficult subject. It is a healthy antidote to the prevailing views, which tend toward either legalism or antinomianism, by grounding the whole subject in the gospel. I heartily recommend this book."
   Jerry Bridges, Author, **The Pursuit of Holiness**

CPSIA information can be obtained at www.ICGtesting.com
Printed in the USA
BVOW022049040113

309717BV00007B/15/P